FINANCIALLY
IRRESPONSIBLE

FINANCIALLY
IRRESPONSIBLE

By

Rahkim Sabree

Copyright 2019 © Unlimited Investment Solutions
All rights reserved.

ISBN-10: 1-7326205-1-3

ISBN-13: 978-1-7326205-1-3

Please visit www.rahkimsabree.com for more information regarding
our programs.

Instagram: @unlimitedinvestmentinquiries

Twitter: finance_fridays

TABLE OF CONTENTS

FOREWORD

By
Geo Derice

"Look at this guy coming down the aisle of the auditorium with his navy-blue sweater on, I wonder who he is, and what he is here for." Those were the first words that came to mind upon meeting Rahkim Sabree on October 26th, 2018. We were part of an event called "Building A Better Brother Summit" in Queens, NY. Rahkim was there from his home near Hartford, Connecticut, three hours away, to pour into the lives of young men the value of mentorship.

I got a chance to speak with him on mentoring myself and I'm blessed to be living large due to the mentoring I received from people who had it in their heart to pay it forward to others. This would be a principle I would later find out to be a foundational one for Rahkim. But that is not what impressed me most about Rahkim, and not why I'm writing this foreword today. What impressed me the most about Rahkim was his discipline, forward thinking, and care for others at the young age of twenty-nine. In just a conversation with him about his desire to see people thriving instead of surviving and helping to pay forward the help and wisdom he got from others, I was instantly attracted and wanted to develop a relationship with him.

As we began to talk, I learned some incredible things such as the non-profit he started to help those impacted by homelessness, to the 800 plus credit score he has and how he acquired it through living "financially irresponsible." His methods and strategies blew me away, so much that I grabbed his arm, twisted it, and made him say uncle until he agreed to let me work alongside him to make sure what you are about to read gets published and into the hands of as many people as possible.

You see, financial freedom is something that has escaped many black and brown folks not because the desire to have it isn't there, but because an example, a model, someone we can relate to has yet to experience it fully or even at all. Before speaking to Rahkim about his desire to help more young minorities experience what it is to strategically play the money game and win, I always thought that financial freedom was for those who look like Suze Orman and Dave Ramsey. I did not know of anyone who grew up from humble beginnings and in neighborhoods like mine playing the money game and winning. When Rahkim shared with me that he owned a multi-family home before he hit thirty years old, my mind was blown. In this book, you'll be inspired, empowered, and given some tools to help you turn what was once a fantasy into a reality. As you read in this book, it's not the ten commandments to financial freedom, nor is it a magic potion that you can glance over and have financial freedom come to you. What this book is, however, is a tale, a true one about someone like you, who is not far removed from you, speaking on what it took for him to get to where he is now, and what it still takes to make sure he stays there. This book you're holding did not have to be published, but as you'll know after reading this book, that's just not who Rahkim Sabree is. Rahkim is not about standing at the top of a mountain only to find himself there. He's the type of young man who believes financial freedom is a team sport and a journey best traveled together.

It's my hope that you do not just read some of this book or dismiss any part of the book because it is all relevant to the big picture of financial freedom. The money game is one that you can win when you adopt the ideas and suggestions Rahkim shares within this book. As you read this book, begin to think of what can be, instead of what has been, think of the wins to come and overlook the losses that have passed. You are about to embark on an important journey and the coolest thing is you do not have to travel it alone. Let Rahkim mentor you toward living your best life, you won't regret it!

INTRODUCTION
PART 1

You're probably thinking, here's yet another book on financial literacy. More "guru" advice to tell me how I am supposed to "build wealth" and manage my money. All the reasons why I need to start now instead of later and how the only barrier to my success is my mindset and attitude.

You're not entirely wrong.

In fact, if you're at all familiar with the work I do, you know that I am adamant and passionate about making people realize that it starts with you ... whatever "it" is.

A better body, good health, good credit, building wealth, etc.

Financial literacy has become quite the buzzword especially when addressing the millennial population. However, I feel that there is something missing when it comes to the conversation about it. REPRESENTATION.

Representation matters and often the people who are sharing the information are not and have not been in the shoes of the ones who are asking to receive the information. In other cases, people will share information that they've heard was a good strategy without having fully applied the methodology to realize success or failure. Representation doesn't only apply to someone's financial past or present, cultural nuances MUST be acknowledged when the exchange of experiences occurs, particularly when addressing so called "minorities".

As I began writing this book, I had to take into consideration the current landscape when it comes to financial empowerment (empowerment distinctly different from literacy) and the conversation around financial literacy (more on the difference later) and honestly ask myself if what I have to say adds to the conversation or is it just white noise that no one will benefit from? I was concerned with "oversaturating" the market; that my words would be lost in the vacuum of all things finance related. I was worried about credibility.

When I became conscious of the fact that people were bought into and amazed by the attitude I carried, strategies executed, and the results of my own financial empowerment journey, I realized not only can I add to the conversation, but I'm obligated to do so. "Financially Irresponsible" is the answer to that charge.

This book is a financial empowerment book. Financially empowering because I address spiritual myths, mindset, and practical application of strategies and information. As three degrees—spiritual, mental, and physical—are addressed, the information herein has the potential to be life-changing. What you're holding in your hand is a series of perspectives, strategies, and experiences that are unique to me and have helped in creating the relationship that I currently have with my personal finances. Like all relationships, it's not perfect and it continues to change. What worked for me yesterday may not work today. It requires sacrifice, discipline, and nurturing. Lastly, It's unique to me. My goal in writing this book was to simply provide perspective and add value to others in a realistic, relatable way when it comes to personal finance. It's not my intention to tell you WHAT to do with your finances, but to simply give you the inspiration to do SOMETHING.

Over nearly ten years, I've had the opportunity to engage with financial education in various capacities. Through financial services/banking, entrepreneurial endeavors (both my own and others), education on investing styles, types, and strategies, as well as one-on-one financial mentorship.

One of the things I've noticed spanning many conversations is that there are too many people who either don't know how to manage their finances, or don't believe in their ability to effectively manage or improve their financial situation. The reality is, lots of people are negatively impacted by their lack of relationship with personal finance or simply understanding money.

With financial literacy being in vogue, I saw this as an opportunity to step out and contribute wherever the conversation is relevant. Whether it be in the arena of homelessness prevention, the rise of consumer debt and debt elimination, student loan debt, or simply at home budgeting, my hope is to exchange and engage. In addition, the increased access to information makes it easy to consume, discuss, refer, or share best practices. Now more than ever your financial destiny is in your hands if you're willing to make something out of it.

But you don't know what you don't know.

That's why I strive to close the gap with my platform and share the techniques I've witnessed, observed, and applied to my own financial management with others who may not have had the same levels of exposure that I have.

What Makes This Book Different?

The INTENT. This book is not to be viewed as a textbook. It's not religious or spiritual law. It's a conversation starter, an agitator. The title, "Financially Irresponsible" was designed to provide inspiration of an alternative story on what your relationship with personal finance and money can look like. My intentions are solely to share with you examples of what I've done and show you how they can be applied to your financial situation.

WARNING!

Some of the strategies and practices I've employed could be viewed as financially irresponsible and unorthodox. My strategies may challenge what you believe about money management and may tempt you to make decisions that are financially irresponsible. Let me go on record as stating I do not accept any liability resulting from a reader's attempt to duplicate, imitate, or otherwise misquote what I discuss here as financial advice. Anyone attempting said strategies is doing so of their own free will against my direction and thus shall be solely liable.

Now that that's out of the way Here's a question I have for you to ponder before we take off on our financial journey:

Reflection Question:

Are you being financially irresponsible by just accepting what is status quo and not challenging what's always been told to you?

Here's who this book is not for or for who this book may not add much value for:

The closed minded—those who, after reading my work. will remain unchanged and unmotivated to believe in themselves.

Licensed and unlicensed financial professionals, financial academics, and people with a sound financial education viewing this through the vein of their experiences—you'll likely feel there's nothing I can tell you. You might be right; you might be wrong. However, without an open mind the book won't do much for adding value to you.

People looking for a get rich quick formula—sorry you won't find that here.

Then Who is This Book For?

ANYONE can draw inspiration or insight from this text; however, I wrote this book with a specific audience in mind. Those who are twenty-one to thirty-five years old entering their careers or slightly established. Old enough to have made a financial mistake or two, but young enough to rebound and recover. I also wrote for those who didn't benefit from a foundation where financial education has been afforded, due simply to the need to survive. I wrote it for the so-called minorities and diasporic Africans who have been left to repeat cycles of poverty around the world.

If you've never had exposure to financial education, have experienced poverty, have not had role models who have a healthy and positive relationship with their personal finances, then this book is for you. If you are someone who has lost hope of owning and controlling your finances, this book is for you. If you're struggled through the cycle of living paycheck to paycheck wondering if this maze has an exit door, this book is for you. If you're in the beginning stages of planning for your future or are conscious of the financial needs you will have in the future, this book is for you. Lastly, if you just need some encouragement around what IS possible, then this book is for you.

Who is Rahkim Sabree and Why Should I Listen to Him?

At the time of writing this book, Rahkim Sabree is a Millennial Black Entrepreneur who at under the age of thirty has accomplished things financially many either dream to or have long given up on. He's attained and exceeded the 800 credit score, purchased and owns a multi-family home, and also has started two businesses, one of which he's co-founded as a not-for-profit that works to help combat homelessness among people currently impacted by homelessness, those at risk of homelessness, the working poor, at risk youth, and other issues that plague many from inner-city backgrounds.

Rahkim Sabree is someone who is:

+ Authentic
+ Concerned with the world at large
+ Responsible and accountable for his own reality and fate.

He is not somebody who has "made it." He's not writing this book to you from an ivory tower with no concept of what it's like to be poor. He's someone who has been in the trenches you are in right now and understands the struggle. What struggle? Struggles like living in Section 8 housing. Struggles like waiting for the food stamp balance to be replenished at the beginning of the month. Struggles like having to search for quarters to do laundry or end up hand washing clothes in the bathroom sink and hanging them to dry overnight on the shower rod.

You might be thinking, isn't this an inspirational book about finances? Yes, it is, but without sharing how relatable his story truly is, very few would understand the magnitude of the climb out of it.

The Wrap Up

As you can see, I have quite the resume, and much more to accomplish! Today I stand before you as someone who is financially confident. That confidence is empowering. Imagine walking into any car dealership or anywhere that's requiring good credit to make a purchase decision and not having to think twice about whether or not you would be approved on the basis of score. Imagine having an income generating strategy in place for retirement. Imagine being able to move about with the confidence of a safety net. The state of my financial affairs puts me in a place of power, a place where I feel like the victor and not the victim. It has even afforded me the ability to do what people would consider being "financially irresponsible."

Here's what you as the reader can expect to learn as a result of reading this book:

✓ Basic financial terms and strategies

✓ A mindset shift

✓ Personal financial hacks

✓ My story and experiences

WHEN you are done reading this book, you will have a foundation for:

✓ Greater control, confidence, and empowerment over your finances

✓ A starting point for building on your own financial acumen

✓ A better sense of vision in terms of what you can do

✓ An increased desire to learn more so you can shape outcomes in the ways you desire

It is my hope that by reading this book, you will face head on your fears and anxieties when it comes to your relationship with your finances and therefore understand money for what it truly is, a tool.

CHAPTER 1
MONEY IS NOT THE ROOT OF ALL EVIL

"For the love of money is the root of all evil: which while some coveted after, they have erred from the faith, and pierced themselves through with many sorrows."

1 Timothy: 6:10 King James Bible

HAVE YOU EVER HEARD A particular saying over and over again from multiple sources? Generally stated, most people (even in the face of evidence that contradicts it) will assume and even swear that there is truth in that saying.

For years people have carefully maneuvered around the subject of money and the desire to accumulate it for fear of being thought of or associated with "evil." Growing up, I often heard the phrase "money is the root of all evil," as a cautionary reference to the 1 Timothy quote I opened this chapter with. In fact, I'm certain many of you have heard the phrase in passing as well. However, the phrase and the Bible quotation are not one in the same. Where the phrase calls attention to money itself being the root of evil, the quotation speaks to the love of money, and there is a stark difference between the two.

Like a game of telephone, I believe what happened over time is that people repeated the term or tried summarizing it and leaving out crucial elements of the text while still accepting it as law. For many, in an attempt to walk a more noble path, the acquisition of money was put to the side as it's often accepted that instead "God will provide." This is not said in jest or to condemn or convert. It is truly the belief held by a population of people that in total devotion to their "Most High," or God, there will be reciprocation in this physical world and in the hereafter. How's that for delayed gratification?

In my opinion, the spirit of that specific text comes down to speaking of greed, or a lust of the heart, more so than money itself being the root of evil.

Many times, the acquisition of money itself is not the end goal. The acquisition of money does things for people. It allows them to live life on their terms. In that way, money serves as a tool to free people in their expression or pursuit of their life's purpose. Money provides the farmer with his tools and seed; it provides the builders with tools to create institutions of learning; it funds the staffing of teachers and other essential professionals so that they can perform life-changing and life-saving actions for man. However, money also provides the means to fund war, oppress others, and simply become consumed with making more money!

Money, like any tool, requires training, awareness of its potential impact, and conscious direction. Think sharp knife, think loaded firearm, or plugged in power tool; most people are not wielding these tools without a training or awareness in how it's used, even if they choose to use them for wrong.

As I open up this section and chapter with spirit, it's important and necessary to underscore the significance of the spiritual and mental relationship that exists, and is often neglected, when it comes to money. You see, money represents an idea. It's an energy source of sorts. With that energy source, there is an exchange like a current (hence the term currency). There is a direct correlation between your beliefs about money and your physical experience with money. I'm not saying that you can affirm a million dollars will land on your doorstep, but I am saying if you don't believe you can ever reach millionaire status, you won't. So regarding the idea that "God will provide;" what if God IS providing and you're simply talking yourself out of it by what you believe about yourself or tell yourself every day?

"I'm broke."

"I can't afford it."

"I can't save."

"That's not for me"

"In another life..."

If you don't believe in a God per se, but rather rely on simple science, how psychologically traumatic is it to hear over and over in your own voice that you can't do something? Or that something isn't for you. You hear something enough times and it becomes part of your reality.

It's interesting to note that the people who are considered the most "greedy" are also some of the most ambitious. That ambition often starts from a place of lack. The slow and steady overcoming of obstacles, or simply making moves from a place of trauma or survival. Think about how many ambitious people ended up in a life of crime. They may be considered unethical or immoral due to the nature of their pursuits or ambition being misinterpreted. And that's not to excuse the deeds of criminals, it simply points to a possible place of origin for their crimes. They say: "The road to hell is paved with good intentions."

I look at the people who are celebrated as some of the richest people in the world today—Jeff Bezos, Elon Musk, even Bill Gates. These people don't have to worry about going to a job every day. They don't have to worry about survival. They have the freedom to make a difference on a global scale. They get not only to live in their purpose, but to determine what their purpose is. How many of us can say the same?

So how do we break from the negative stigma associated with acquiring money and begin to live the lives of those who effectively use money as a tool? Well, first we have to give up this "broke but woke" mentality.

(I did not coin that phrase, by the way.)

We can be noble, disciplined, authentic to ourselves and our communities, and still pursue a better quality of life by understanding how money works, and by making money work for us.

Robert Kiyosaki stated, "The European system of education creates two kinds of people, SOLDIERS and EMPLOYEES; people who take orders."

In his book, Rich Dad, Poor Dad, Kiyosaki explores the difference between a standard education and a financial one. Ninety-nine percent of my readers are going to have a hard time recalling a financial education curriculum during schooling and that's because one likely didn't exist. That is another reason why it's my personal charge to share what it is I've overheard, witnessed, learned, applied, and continue to study with anyone and everyone I can.

On the topic of "broke but woke," we have to move away from allowing spiritual institutions to be the recipient of financial contributions over our own well-being and the well-being of our households. I'm not stating that giving to charity, be it a spiritual institution like a church, temple, or mosque, or an organization relying on community donations to provide needed work is a negative thing. As previously mentioned, I co-founded one such organization and those donations are the backbone of our livelihood. What I am saying is that you can't pour from an empty glass. If it's between paying your light bill and paying your church tithes, I hope you are paying your light bill. I'm sorry to say, you simply cannot buy your way into heaven. But what if you can afford to do both? That's fantastic. However, there is an order of operations I like to apply when it comes to the distribution of my income and it starts with paying myself first. This is a strategy I'm going to dive into a bit deeper later on in the book; however, do know that no bill, expense, or financial obligation is met before I pay myself first.

> **"If you build yourself to a place where you have wealth, you can share that wealth to make a difference." —Rahkim Sabree**

Bill Gates is known as one of the world's foremost philanthropists. Bill Gates through the Bill and Melinda

Gates foundation has the ability to change and impact people's lives by using the money he has acquired. Had he not acquired wealth for himself, his contributions simply would not be possible. Some records show that the foundation has donated more than thirty-six billion dollars to charitable causes. Talk about making a difference!

Too many people blindly allocate their money into every priority but their future.

What about you?

You deserve it.

You are worth it.

I'm not taking about spending extra on getting your nails and hair done or getting the latest and greatest from Macy's or the Apple store. I'm talking about building a financial base that will give you greater wiggle room in the event of an emergency or an opportunity comes up for you to grow your money. I'm talking about being in a position to make a difference in one life or many without having to worry about how this is going to impact your own financial well-being. I'm sure many of us have "given up our last" to someone we deemed as needing it more. What if we don't have to give up our last? What if we can simply give?

Aspiring to Be Poor

I often open up discussions on my personal financial journey with the statement that I aspired to be poor. I know it sounds weird, but this mindset is one that does plague many people when it comes to their relationship with money. Of course, I didn't literally want to be poor. What I mean when I say this is based on the behaviors I'd observed growing up and becoming aware of the financial situation in the household, I thought what I was accustomed to was what success looked like. Especially for a young black man growing up in Mount Vernon, New York. I thought "making it" was getting food stamps and being approved for Section 8 housing. I could have my own apartment and I'd be on my way! I never considered that I could afford to buy groceries on my own or that instead of getting a small one-bedroom apartment, I could own a house. I remember becoming so aware of household finances that in anticipation of being told no, I would often ask for the least expensive viable object when my parents would ask me what I wanted for my birthday or holidays. Imagine how I had to retrain my brain to believe and accept a limitless possibility, or rather "the impossibility of impossibility," as I like to call it.

Contrary to the sentiment about the "love of money" mentioned in the Bible, I believe that not only can't we afford to not acquire money, but that we actually have a responsibility to do so.

14 "For the kingdom of heaven is like a man traveling to a far country, who called his own servants and delivered his goods to them. 15 And to one he gave five talents, to another two, and to another one, to each according to his own ability; and immediately he went on a journey. 16 Then he who had received the five talents went and traded with them, and made another five talents. 17 And likewise he who had received two gained two more also. 18 But he

who had received one went and dug in the ground, and hid his lord's money. 19 After a long time the lord of those servants came and settled accounts with them.

20 "So he who had received five talents came and brought five other talents, saying, 'Lord, you delivered to me five talents; look, I have gained five more talents besides them.' 21 His lord said to him, 'Well done, good and faithful servant; you were faithful over a few things, I will make you ruler over many things. Enter into the joy of your lord.' 22 He also who had received two talents came and said, 'Lord, you delivered to me two talents; look, I have gained two more talents besides them.' 23 His lord said to him, 'Well done, good and faithful servant; you have been faithful over a few things, I will make you ruler over many things. Enter into the joy of your lord.'

24 "Then he who had received the one talent came and said, 'Lord, I knew you to be a hard man, reaping where you have not sown, and gathering where you have not scattered seed. 25 And I was afraid, and went and hid your talent in the ground. Look, there you have what is yours.'

26 "But his lord answered and said to him, 'You wicked and lazy servant, you knew that I reap where I have not sown, and gather where I have not scattered seed. 27 So you ought to have deposited my money with the bankers, and at my coming I would have received back my own with interest. 28 So take the talent from him, and give it to him who has ten talents.

29 "For to everyone who has, more will be given, and he will have abundance; but from him who does not have, even what he has will be taken away. 30 And cast the

unprofitable servant into the outer darkness. There will be weeping and gnashing of teeth."

Matthew 25: 14-29 King James Bible

That series of verses speaks to me in terms of the potential and power we possess. Whatever your spiritual views, we have an obligation to leave this existence having created more than we came into it with. One of the ways we can do this is with money.

"If you're making money and you're choosing not to grow that money, grow an opportunity, or take your talents and monetize them, you are doing yourself a disservice."

— RAHKIM SABREE

CHAPTER 2
THE POVERTY MINDSET

"O SON OF SPIRIT!

I created thee rich, why dost thou bring thyself down to poverty?

Noble I made thee, wherewith dost thou abase thyself? Out of the essence of knowledge I gave thee being, why seekest thou enlightenment from anyone beside Me? Out of the clay of love I molded thee, how dost thou busy thyself with another? Turn thy sight unto thyself, that thou mayest find Me standing within thee, mighty, powerful, and self-subsisting."

(The Hidden Words of Baha'u'llah)

IN THE LAST CHAPTER, WE discussed the idea that money is a tool we can use to responsibly take care of ourselves first, and that by taking care of ourselves we can then help others. That it is not the "root of all evil."

So why do so many people place money on this pedestal? I remember one day I went to a seminar and there were a significant number of people who had money. The featured speaker at this event started off by telling the story of her climb to wealth and how now, "making money was fun!"

I was offended in an instant.

She went on to say that after she made her first $250,000, how quickly she was able to make her first million. It was "so easy" to keep making money she said. The audience cheered and agreed, she segued into a sales pitch for her product (that will save time and teach you how to make money or something of the sort), and I just sat there stupefied.

I was offended because in that moment I thought of the many instances in which making money was not fun and when having no money was even less fun. I was offended knowing how many crimes are committed and lives locked away in the pursuit of money. I was offended because I knew how much stress and anxiety surrounds making money. How many opportunities I've missed due to my family not having money. All of the short cuts I've had to learn to make money spread. The emphasis my mom would place on finishing our plates because "there are kids in Africa starving." Walking the extra mile to the other grocery store because their prices were cheaper. Hand washing clothes in the bathroom sink with dish detergent because we didn't have laundry detergent and no change to put into the washing machines at the laundromat up the block. When I finally snapped out of it, I wrote down her statement, quietly gathered my things, and left during the sales pitch. I didn't walk out of that room discouraged; I left that room determined to find the fun in making money. I also left the room questioning why her statement triggered such a strong emotional reaction in me.

I touched briefly on the power of belief in the previous chapter. It's very hard to have a healthy relationship with money if you are living with what is called a "Poverty Mindset."

"Beliefs can so color our minds that we become paralyzed, unable to move beyond our fears and doubts, thus limiting our choices. Blind to our potential, we wander aimlessly, searching for enlightenment, yet remain barred from the infinite possibilities that are all around us."

DR. JOY DEGRUY (POST TRAUMATIC SLAVE SYNDROME)

Before breaking down the Poverty Mindset, it's important first to define poverty, and then understand the root of the word. Poverty actually comes from the old French word Poverte referring to a 'wretched condition or state.' So you see, poverty in its essence is less a reflection of your financial holdings and more a reflection of your state of mind.

"Poverty is not a reflection of wealth or lack of wealth, but more so referring to what your state of being is, which could be narrowed down to your mindset."

—RAHKIM SABREE

When we talk about the Poverty Mindset, it's important to break down that word, because you can be without money and not have a Poverty Mindset. Inversely, you can win the lottery, become a multimillionaire and maintain a Poverty Mindset. As a result, that mindset will dictate whether or not you attract opportunities to make money, or you avoid them. (Think conscious direction from the previous chapter.)

The Poverty Mindset is often characterized by scarcity, which speaks to this idea that "there will never be enough." With a Scarcity Mindset you are concerned with surviving today and just "maintaining" until the next thing comes along. The next bill, the next paycheck, the next expense, etc., so that you can scramble to "make ends meet," or "rob Peter to pay Paul."

I use quotations around these phrases as I'm sure you've either heard or uttered those words yourself. This scarcity includes the concept of hoarding or trying to save everything that you have with the intentions of holding on to it just in case. We are often taught to save money without context on what exactly we are saving for. That's like stockpiling ammunition without knowing how to load a weapon. Sure, having it on hand gives you a sense of security, but are you ever truly prepared to use it? When we stockpile money, we're disrupting the flow of currency. While I won't discourage the discipline of saving, most people don't realize that saving money is like cupping water in your hands. What you end up with, often isn't the same as what you started with. This is due primarily to inflation. With economic inflation, there is a general increase in prices and a fall in the purchasing value of money. Remember the twenty-five-cent bag of potato chips you grew up on that now costs fifty cents for the same bag? That's inflation. Your twenty-five cents has less purchasing power today than it did yesterday.

The Poverty Mindset also refers to demonstrations of wealth that we see frequently on social media and on TV. We consume that behavior and try to emulate it, often to our detriment. We opt to purchase liabilities or things that give us little to no return on investment yet steer clear of assets or things that can make us money because it's "boring" or "complicated." One of our peers has the newest and nicest, so we have to get the newest and nicest to keep up. We can't seem to get into the habit of putting money aside because there is never enough, but somehow, we have a new outfit to go out in every weekend.

The Poverty Mindset speaks to the attitudes, behaviors, and beliefs we hold toward our relationship with money as individuals, as families, and as communities.

"Our families and communities model for us how to be, who to play with. They teach us about power: who has it, (and that it is almost never them), and how to live, love and survive without it."

—Dr. Joy DeGruy

We discussed the power of words earlier. More specifically, we discussed the impact of the words we use directed to ourselves. The message I want to drill into your head before you leave this section is that the words we use, shape our reality. On your journey to becoming more financially responsible, you MUST control what you allow yourself to believe about yourself and your potential.

Here are some root causes of a Poverty Mindset and my hope is to provide solutions or actionable items to address them by the end of this book:

A Lack of Financial Education, Learned Helplessness, or Having to Exist in Survival Mode

We do not choose the circumstances by which we enter this world, but we certainly have the ability to choose how we navigate it and what we accomplish before we leave it. Financial education is often not taught in our school systems and in the so-called minority communities it's not discussed at home either. As a reader of this book, you have either made a choice to change that dynamic for yourself and your family already or are preparing to do so. Financial education involves continuous learning as the financial landscape of the world changes. This is a commitment and it's not one you have to make alone, but you do have to make it.

"Generational Curses"

There's a lot of buzz around this concept of breaking or destroying "generational curses." But to take the spook factor out of it ... "generational curses" refers to settling for what is the status quo, or behaviors and mentalities unconsciously passed down, which keep you restrained. These can refer to a host of things like the relationships we form, our dietary preferences, or our beliefs about money. So when you talk about breaking a "generational curse," what you're really talking about is changing your behavior, changing your mentality, or your approach to managing money, or whatever it is that you're prone to. It could be abuse, it could be an addiction, it could be a dysfunction. Someone is changing the mentality and the behaviors around that particular thing. I believe it was Einstein who's credited with saying, "The definition of insanity is doing the same thing over and over and expecting a different result." I believe the same to be true with poor financial management.

Before I move to the next point, I need to revisit something quickly. I mentioned that in breaking the "generational curse" you're changing YOUR behavior, YOUR mentality, YOUR approach. However, you're not just doing it for you. By 'breaking the curse' you are drawing a line in the sand and deciding that for future generations you will set the tone for a new behavior, a new mentality, and a new approach. Breaking "generational curses" is bigger than you.

The Fear of Success

I've observed that people typically feel comfortable with what they know and what they're familiar with. So building on the concept of "generational curses," you are assuming the burden of challenging what was the norm across, at the very least, one generation, but more often than not, several. Going against the grain can be scary. I discuss fear in a future chapter; however, what you won't find when you survey people like you, and me, and others who have experienced poverty, is a willingness to admit to being fearful of success. Success can be defined in many ways and however you define it, you will certainly wear it. Success draws the attention of others. Sometimes even burdens you with guilt and a sense of obligation. As a trail blazer, you may be ridiculed, taunted, or even made fun of in the beginning stages. You may be criticized when you slip up, and have your victories considered a fluke. I can admit to my fear of success. In fact, when I started this journey as an author and speaker, I decided to put my face on the cover of my first book, Mentorship: The Playbook. I was terrified.

EVERY. STEP. OF. THE. WAY.

However, I was also courageous. By putting my face on the cover of a book, I had to prepare for people to recognize me, to criticize or ridicule me, and for people to celebrate me. Within my own nucleus of friends and family, I had to set the record straight that I am not the bank of Rahkim Sabree and that while I'm certainly willing to discuss financial strategies, I am in no way willing to part with my money so that bad habits and "generational curses" could be perpetuated. (Do you see what I did there?)

The Responsibility That Comes with Success

So what happens when you overcome your fear? How many times have you heard of an account where someone "forgot where they came from?" Or they, "made it out" but don't ever give back? Giving back is an essential part of being financially responsible. I'm not taking about giving up your money (although there are tax incentives associated with donations). I'm talking about paying it forward. For years now, I have been sharing my journey with close friends and family. Every mistake, every win, every new lesson. Without knowing it, I was building my credibility, but more than that, I was inspiring others. So many joy-filled instances have occurred when someone close to me reaches out in excitement about what they were able to accomplish thanks to my taking the lead and investing my knowledge with them. Financial empowerment is a team sport and the more people you have in your circle who are familiar with the ways to navigate the financial landscape, the more conversations that are had around successes (and failures), the more sharing of information that occurs, the more likely the previous root causes mentioned will be addressed.

> *"The fear of success, fear of wealth, fear of carrying the burden, and leading the way can also deter people from taking steps towards breaking that Poverty Mindset."*
>
> —RAHKIM SABREE

Aspiring to Be Poor Cont'd...

In the previous chapter, I discussed how I often open my talks by saying that I aspired to be poor.

I do this primarily for two reasons:

1. First, to connect to my audience. When I tell these personal stories, people can see themselves, their current circumstances, or maybe their past

circumstances in what it is I've experienced.

2. Shock value. Why? Because that is what grabs people's attention. Many people associate the topic of finances with something boring. So when I go and say something like, "I aspired to be poor," people look at me like I have two heads. I go on to explain that because I didn't have the context or the education I do now about personal financial management, that I was unconsciously striving to move in that direction without even knowing it.

When I became conscious of the household finances—we had Section 8, we had food stamps—I thought that when I became an independent adult that I would want food stamps and Section 8 housing to supplement my income, which for me would have been winning. But why did I think that? I thought that because I would've had assistance. That speaks to the Poverty Mindset that I had as well, because I didn't believe I was even capable in my early twenties to have an income that would be able to support me without aid from these government programs. So that's what I mean when I say "I was aspiring to be poor," because we know that those programs are associated with a lower level of income. And once you break a certain threshold in income, you don't qualify for the program anymore.

It's truly a sad case but there are scenarios where people will shy away from improving themselves, making more money, or avoid finding ways to increase their income to maintain those program benefits. Fortunately, I didn't perpetrate this Poverty Mindset as I grew and became experienced in financial education. But it definitely was something that I had committed to strategy prior to being eighteen years old, or prior to turning twenty-one.

Self-Fulfilling Prophecies

There are two kinds of self-fulfilling prophecies:

1. There is the self-fulfilling prophecy of doing what others expect of you. So if you're constantly told that you're not going to do enough, be anything, achieve anything, you end up in a position where you also know you fulfilled that prophecy based on what their perception is of you, or what others are saying you are and you give up on challenging it.

2. There is also the self-fulfilling prophecy where your expectations of yourself are such that you will not exceed a certain limit or get to a place of true abundance. Everyone around you can be rooting you on with the belief that you are the chosen one! However, as previously discussed, you will only go as far as you believe is possible.

So again, when we discuss poverty and the associated mindset, we know that it truly starts in the mind! I absolutely know that the temptation to be complacent is real, and that it prolongs financial success.

"What's needed to move beyond self-fulfilling prophecies are relevant and intimate examples of how to be more as a successful person."

—RAHKIM SABREE

Building the Mindset of Financially Successful People

First, I would say, educate yourself, and understand money and how it flows. Seek mentorship and model someone else's success. If you can't find somebody who's been able to accomplish the things you're looking to personally accomplish, you can model success through the LESSONS and STORIES of others in text, audio books, and interviews. This is one of the great benefits of living in the information age. It's so easy to get access to information about different strategies people use, specifically around personal finances.

Some of my favorite Finance Powerhouses to Study:

✓ Robert Kiyosaki

✓ Grant Cardone

✓ Dave Ramsey

✓ Garret B. Gunderson

These financial strategists are often regarded as some of the top people associated with having and building wealth. What I don't see on that list, however, are individuals that look like me. So again, representation matters, doesn't it? Why would I believe that I could achieve something that no one who looks like me is celebrated for achieving? That doesn't undermine the work and accomplishments of the likes of Oprah, Michael Jordan, Jay-Z, and others in entertainment and sports. That speaks specifically to people who work from a place of building wealth and teaching others how to build wealth as well. And therein lies my mission.

"Financial strategy involves a specific mindset, quickly followed up by putting systems in place to learn how to make money and continue to make it grow into the future."

—RAHKIM SABREE

"Believe in the impossibility of impossibility."

Essentially, that's suspending the belief that what is considered impossible is unattainable. That anything is possible. Take small actions every day to compound discipline and positive decision making. This is known as the compound effect discussed in the book The Compound Effect by Darren Hardy. Realistically speaking, you're not going to change your financial practices overnight. Despite the journey being challenging, you can do it. Your situation will improve over time if you consistently take small steps, mentally and financially, to change.

I decided recently that I was spending too much money and I wanted more money to invest every pay period. I'm an avid Starbucks shopper and so on my way to work I often stop and buy a drink. A caramel macchiato with no foam, whipped cream, and almond milk (shout out to Mom for putting me on). One day I decided that instead of going to Starbucks to get this drink, I would take the money I'd typically spend and move it into my savings account. Five dollars in the grand scheme of things is not going to make a significant difference in my savings; however, done every day, that five dollars adds up quickly!

"To save money, and believe that you're spending money, mentally trick yourself by moving money into your savings account. This very small habit will compound your money over a long period of time. This mental trick concept can be applied over and over into any area of your life."

—RAHKIM SABREE

I strongly recommend the book mentioned above, The Compound Effect, by Darren Hardy. This book talks about the power of taking small steps and small actions repeatedly over a long period of time and the great results that it yields.

I Just Can't!

Are you a person who cannot live without coffee? Does a caramel macchiato call you the minute your alarm goes off and you're not a person until you have it? What do you do in that case? Are you not to live at all?

Trust me, I'm the same. So how did I do it? I took five dollars and I bought a box of black tea. Instead of drinking the caramel macchiato, I drank a cup of hot tea in the morning. The whole box of black tea cost me the same as one drink from Starbucks. Thinking long term, that whole box of black tea would get me through a couple of weeks. In this case, what I've done is not necessarily cutting out a habit but replacing the habit with a substitute, ultimately creating a new habit loop.

This concept is something discussed in the *Power of Habit* by Charles Duhigg. Essentially, you're keeping that habit loop, but instead of trying to end the habit, you're just replacing that habit with a better habit.

To truly be effective, there has to be a desire there for some kind of change, which means you need to intentionally and consciously initiate the process.

Here's a further breakdown of using Habit Loops with our Starbucks example:

The habit loop, in this case, would be the stimuli of associating "work" with "drinking hot beverages (caramel macchiato)."

Replacement: Instead of going to get the caramel macchiato, you replace the stimuli of getting to work with the reward of a hot beverage, which is now "black tea." As a benefit, you can buy a box of tea for the cost of one caramel macchiato, thus saving you money.

I'm not saying that I haven't on occasion decided to treat myself, take a break, and reward myself with a five-dollar caramel macchiato. But I've effectively created a habit now where I'm spending less money on Starbucks and saving more money over time.

One last tip about overcoming the Poverty Mindset before we go onto Chapter 3. If you want to break the Poverty Mindset, change and/or control your surroundings. That includes people and places. I grew up in an apartment my whole life. So I never consciously or subconsciously desired to live in a house, because that's not what I knew or was familiar with growing up. I thought if it were possible, I had to make tons of money or be much older. Eventually, I started interacting with people who owned houses—people who were my peers—which sparked the desire in me. I always knew that it would be nice to own a house, but what separated my "nice to have" from my "will have" was seeing it done and deciding I wanted to do it. My desire was amplified by the people I was around who had done it.

CHAPTER 3
THE LAW OF ATTRACTION

"Cogito, ergo sum (I think therefore I am),"

—RENE DESCARTES

The power of affirmation, prayer, even chants and spells aren't just the stuff of religious lore or your favorite supernatural story [insert pop culture reference: Harry Potter, Charmed, The Vampire Diaries, etc.]. It is the conscious direction of the will or intent that gives these things power. In some way, deciding in advance that you are going to be wealthy will in essence lead to you becoming wealthy. However, it's more than just making that decision, more than just wishing it would happen, more than reciting it 100 times a day in front of your mirror holding a shiny rock or lucky penny.

It's easy to dismiss this consciously directed will as fantasy or spook-ism, especially when I speak publicly on financial empowerment and the power of your thoughts, your mindset, and overcoming the ill impact of poverty. The idea that you can generate change based on your mental discipline and focus (belief) is often associated with the concept, "The Law of Attraction." Many people become disenchanted with the simplicity of the law and grow frustrated when they figure the law is broken or flawed.

The Law of Attraction is "the ability to attract what we are focusing on into our lives or the act of manifestation via the transmutation of thoughtful concepts into reality." In other words, it's simply "active manifestation." In essence, you're changing your reality based on your own WILL or INTENT.

When it comes to the Law of Attraction, what people often overlook is that the law involves more than wishing, praying, or hoping that your desired outcome will happen. It requires you taking steps toward that outcome and realizing the infinite possibilities that present themselves as a result of those actions.

"Create momentum by taking steps towards your desired outcome."

—Rahkim Sabree

Think of a magnet.

When you think of magnets, you think about how they attract or pull an item that is within its magnetic field. A lot of times we have things that are barriers within our magnetic field. Our fears, learned helplessness, or a Poverty Mindset are all things that create distance between us and financial success. It's why we need to take deliberate actions toward our goals in order to close the gap so that they can enter our magnetic field.

This process often starts with a THOUGHT. But it does not stop there. To amplify or move the dial on your effectiveness, you can do two things:

1) Write it down.

2) Establish a timeline that you would like to see that goal occurring in—whether it be six months, one year, five years, etc.

3) Take steps towards accomplishing that goal.

I can remember seeing a pretty cool saying that fits in with what we are talking about here:

A DREAM written down with a date becomes a GOAL.

A GOAL broken down into steps becomes a PLAN.

A PLAN backed by ACTION becomes REALITY.

When I was twenty-one, I moved to Connecticut and met someone who was close to my age and owned a house and had excellent credit. I decided quickly that if they can, so can I. I didn't think about all of the reasons why I couldn't, and they could, I thought about all of the reasons why they could and so could I. So, I wrote down what my goal was and then created a timeline (which was about five years) and learned everything I could about how to make this a reality. I started saving money and educating myself about credit, I took aggressive actions toward building credit, and continued to ask questions so I could work toward accomplishing that goal. As a result of my initial thought, writing my goal down, creating a timeline and taking steps toward my goal, I was able to accomplish it within, or very close to, my initial time frame.

I actually almost accomplished it sooner than five years and so you learn that things derail you. It is my firm belief that the universe will hear your wishes and desires, will give you a taste of what you're asking for and then test the material you're made of to see how bad you really want it. During that process, I saved up nearly $12,000 for a down payment and lost it all two years before I actually ended up buying my house. But it was the steps that I took toward making it happen that multiplied the opportunities for me, whether it was educational opportunities or being introduced to people who could help me along my journey.

Often times, the very same people who say, "It would be nice to be rich; it would be nice to be able to afford something; it would be nice to not have to live paycheck to paycheck" won't take the steps toward accomplishing it. They've either surrendered to this concept of mystical faith ("It's above me now") or they just don't put in the work, which is really the secret sauce to the Law of Attraction.

"It's easy to create a vision board; it's easy to write down a list of goals; it's easy to talk about what you want to see happen; but, the hard part is the sacrifice, the consistency, the follow-up, the recalibration when you fall off of the path, the dedication and especially the endurance it requires over a long period of time." Rahkim Sabree

Five years into the future at age twenty-one seemed like eons away, but in hindsight ... it flew by in an instant. In fact, I know a person who once said, the five years are going to come anyway, so you might as well work to make your life the best it can be when it arrives.

Words Have Power

I heard a story about how someone was driving and said, "I hope I don't hit the tree, I hope I don't hit the tree." They went on to repeat that over and over again and guess what happened? They hit the tree. The words they spoke were "hit the tree." You might say that they said, "Don't hit the tree," but the words you use are so powerful that you would never want to speak those words at all. You're better off saying, "I've arrived at my destination safely" over and over again. This applies to our finances as well. We discussed negative self-talk earlier. Things like, "I'm broke" or "I can't afford that" should be replaced with "How can I afford that?" or "What can I do to increase my income so that I have more money?" Using positive language and affirming language around finances versus words that are negative, represent reflections of what mental state you are in (or want to be in). Being present and using positive language is going to make a great difference in your train of thought, while ultimately bringing into your magnetic field instances, opportunities, and catalysts that work toward the accomplishment of your goal.

I believe that anything I want, I can achieve, and so far ... I've been able to do that. This concept has had a positive impact on my life as a whole, but specifically on my relationship with money management. When someone thinks on that level, they take more deliberate and responsible actions and practice disciplines around maintaining those actions. It's kind of like when you're an athlete, or health-conscious, right? You go to the gym and make conscious decisions around being active. Often, you're going to choose to fuel your body with the right kinds of foods. Whereas, if you're living a sedentary lifestyle and not active, then you're more prone to eating fast food, or foods that aren't high in nutritional value. As you know, an object in motion stays in motion, whereas an object at rest will stay at rest. I take special care to focus more on the disciplines and the behaviors around maintaining good financial health, awareness, and education ... rather than being careless and throwing all caution to the wind. That's not to say I haven't, or I don't make irrational or irresponsible decisions. I'm human and I'm battling through the trenches just like you likely are.

> *"Believe that anything you want to achieve is possible."*
> —RAHKIM SABREE

When we discussed the fear of success in the previous chapter, I talked about the "burden" that comes with knowing and applying. I spoke of "wearing" your success, and people recognizing it on you. I think it creates an air or impression about me and my finances that draws unwanted attention to me, which sometimes results in some people believing that I have more. That belief allows them to feel entitled to ask me for money, and then get frustrated about either my lack of willingness or lack of capacity to give. I've had some relationships become strained over other people's projections and ideas of the abundance that I have.

> *"There are times where your decisions will lead you on a very lonely path because people don't have the same drive, ambition, or determination to maintain the disciplines that you will. As a result, they will expect that you are their meal ticket out."*
> —RAHKIM SABREE

You have to draw a line and be able to set yourself up first before you can start helping other people. Very often, people take that line personally and then decide to dissociate themselves from you because they feel like you're not sharing. I've also seen people decide to disassociate themselves because they don't feel worthy of being in your company anymore, simply because they're not doing the things that you're doing.

Exercise (Give This a Try)

Famous actor Jim Carrey talked about how he wrote himself a check for a specific amount and dated it a number of years into the future. When that time elapsed, he actually acquired the amount he wrote down on that check, effectively manifesting it. Talk about Law of Attraction! So I've actually put the same practice into play. I wrote myself a check for a specific amount and dated it ten years into the future and folded it up. I carry it with me in my wallet as a reminder/attractor toward achieving that goal. I'm interested in knowing if you believe enough to do the same? Feel free to contact me via my website (RahkimSabree. com) or social media and let me know how it plays out.

"Take steps every day, deliberate steps, toward making your goal happen."

—RAHKIM SABREE

I've already conceptualized that manifestation in my mind. I've already written it down as a goal, and I've already established a timeline. So now I need to figure out what additional actions need to be taken toward generating income for acquiring assets. Which in turn will put me in a position to meet that specified number. You can do this too for whatever financial goal you have.

I opened up this chapter with a quote from the French Philosopher, Descartes that says, "I think therefore I am." Descartes was a philosopher determined to disprove his existence. He ultimately came to the conclusion that because he can conceptualize the idea of disproving his existence, it confirmed that he actually did exist. What you think, you become. Cogito, ergo sum.

> *"As above so below, as within so without."*
> *"If you really take the time to think about yourself in the grand scheme of things on a micro and macro level of existence ... how you feel about yourself and what you're capable of internally is going to have a profound influence on what you manifest externally."*
> —RAHKIM SABREE

So I emphasize, the Law of Attraction is more than hoping and wishing that something is going to happen, or even just writing it down. I say this because you can practice these exercises in vain if in your heart and mind you don't believe that it's possible. Start from INSIDE of you and have the audacity to really believe in the 'impossibility of impossibility' and then take the steps toward proving that, not for anyone else's gratification but your own.

> *"What you believe about yourself and what you're capable of internally is going to have a direct impact and effect on what you are able to manifest and accomplish externally."*
> —RAHKIM SABREE

CHAPTER 4
FEAR, EXCUSES, AND NOT HAVING ENOUGH TIME

"Too many people are thinking of security instead of opportunity. They seem to be more afraid of life than death."

—James F. Byrnes

I have a question for you.

Is reaching your financial goals important to you?

If you've been reading for this long, then I know the answer but humor me and answer this question for yourself:

On a scale of one to ten. how important is you attaining financial empowerment?

If it's not a seven or above, we have work to do.

"If it is important to you, you will find a way. If not, you'll find an excuse".

When it comes to people asking me how I got an 800 credit score, started two businesses, or purchased a multi-family home, I always ask if they want the simple answer? I don't do excuses. In fact, in The Magic of Thinking Big, there is a chapter dedicated to excuses alone, titled "Cure yourself of Excusitis, The Failure Disease." If you are going to succeed at anything really, it's important to not pack your excuses.

Here are the most frequent excuses I've heard when it comes to mastering money:

"I'm Not Good at Math."

When people think about the tedious disciplines that come with managing your money, they immediately shy away. They believe their ability to manage money through the use of math cannot be done and the thought can discourage or intimidate them from wanting to even pursue it.

"I Don't Have Time."

You MAKE time for what is important to you. Personal financial management can appear intimidating, because very often it's a boring, repetitive, in your face task. People often don't make the time for something that's not going to entertain them.

"I Can't Afford It."

This one speaks to the concept of people either investing in themselves, saving more, or budgeting in such a way that they have the ability to pay themselves first.

There's a man who has his own t-shirt business, and he really wants to get it up and running, but he thinks he doesn't have the ability to pay himself first. After paying all of his bills and barely being able to invest in his t-shirt business, he has nothing left. Probing his situation, a little bit more, I found out that he's a really big smoker, spending a significant amount of money on cigarettes. I pointed out to him that the cigarettes are not necessary, and maybe he could decrease the frequency in which he smokes to save more money, or he could pay himself first before he starts spending money on cigarettes. To find middle ground in his situation, if he wanted to reward himself with what's left over AFTER paying himself first and paying his bills and investing in his business, he certainly could! That would be a better model, instead of trying to figure out how he's going to pay himself after he did everything else. After sharing more with him, he acknowledged that it made sense and he knew what he needed to do but he didn't have the discipline to do so.

"The System is Designed For Us to Fail."

This one is a favorite of mine so I'm very adamant about including this specific commentary. The deck is stacked against us. Institutional racism, predatory lending, redlining, school to prison pipeline, affirmative action, gentrification, diversity and inclusion, capitalism, etc. are all terms we've heard of historically and/or today. Although these factors are undeniable and make it difficult if not impossible to navigate the political and economic landscapes, that does not mean we give up. It means we get creative. It means we get educated. We learn to play the game.

When I hear these things from people, they are valid concerns and reflections of the environment they live in. However, what people must realize is that they do have the power internally to control their perception, their actions, their behaviors, and their education in navigating through what barriers are present by working together to build wealth. What I've personally accomplished is not at all by accident. All of it was planned, strategized over, and executed on. I want people to realize that I'm very well aware of the fact that certain situations I've been able to avoid or situations I have not encountered based on how I was positioned by my family, by my friends, by certain decisions I've made around my life path, and I'm not immune to the barriers listed above. I'm more adept at navigating the landscape, simply because I understand aspects of the game that are not often taught. Aspects of the game that I'm sharing with you now.

I had this experience where I went in to buy a new car and I find myself being profiled immediately. There is no regard to what my credit score is or how much cash I have in my pocket. I could tell by the language, the tone, and the dismissive nature of the sales rep that they thought I was wasting their time. I had a similar scenario occur after purchasing my home where I went to purchase furniture at a furniture store and the clerk tells me that the furniture set I want to purchase is not in stock and I would not be able to get it delivered for a week. He proceeds to offer me financing through the store to which I decline and pull out my American Express credit card. How quickly their attitude and tone changed. They literally followed me around the store, waiting on me hand and foot and somehow found a way to get this furniture set delivered to me the next day based on the fact that they realized I'm credit worthy. Fortunately in both scenarios, I had the means financially to support my purchasing decision. But, what about those who aren't in the position I was?

Why should anyone have to experience negligent sales practices or blatant disrespect based on these internalized or institutionalized racist structures. They shouldn't! However, I was able to navigate through it by being empowered.

"It's Too Risky."

There is an ever-present risk in ignorance. I once heard the quote: "There is no bad investment, just bad investors." When there is a lack of education present, everything is risky. So we talked about hoarding your savings and the concept of inflation earlier, let me ask you: Is it more or less risky to stack money in a savings account earning less than three percent when the rate of inflation is exceeding the return on your interest rate effectively costing you money over time? Or is it better to invest your money in the stock market, where, true there is much more volatility and no insurance, but historically over time you realize five to nine percent of a return? Is it riskier to walk down the street on the sidewalk, drive down the highway, or fly in the air? There's risk in everything. You're taking the risk any which way. So long as your risk is an informed risk, an educated risk, then it really takes some of the risk out of it because you're able to then predict the outcome from a place of education instead of fear or just hoping for the best. Now, I've made my disclaimer at the beginning of this book around my perspective being just that and not financial advice. However, let me go further and say that I am not in any way discouraging the accumulation of money in a FDIC insured savings vehicle. What I am doing, is challenging your thoughts and perceptions around "security" by hoarding, or worse, by not saving at all!

"Fear" - The Legitimate Excuse

Fear comes in many forms, especially when it comes to finances. One major form is the fear of failure, a fear of not being able to provide, or fear of poverty. These are all fears I've navigated and I'm sure you have too. Especially if you have people who depend on you. Fear paralyzes you. It's kind of like what happens when the deer jumps out in the middle of the night on the highway and they get caught in the glare of the headlight and freeze because they're paralyzed with fear. Instead of continuing to move and maybe not getting hit, they stand there and get hit anyway. I think that's what happens a lot of times with people. They are allowing the fear to direct them into not making a decision and they're still on this collision course instead of trying some maneuver out of it.

I like to say that poor people are the second most innovative fundraisers on the planet. Who are the first? Children. Children command so much wealth when it comes to the things that they want; the gifts they receive, and even the clothes they wear. Whether it be for the holidays like birthdays and Christmas or for school shopping, children often get what they want. And so if we can harness the ability of children to command wealth or the ability to raise funds and direct it into an asset and not liability, then we can start to initiate wealth building at a very young age. By leveraging their uncanny ability to fundraise, we can teach them how to make money work for them. I can't tell you how many instances I've witnessed either growing up or as an adult, personally or peripherally, where parents "make a way." Even my own parents, somehow, someway, were able to make things happen for my siblings and I.

Now, we didn't have the matching name brand outfits or every pair of Jordan's known to man, but on the very special occasions we would get the latest and greatest in electronics (I got the first generation PlayStation portable one year and the PlayStation 2 that I had to share with my brother another year) or some other action figure of the day. (My brother and I had all our favorite WWE, formally WWF, action figures complete with entrance stage and fighting ring!)

I say poor people are the second most innovative fundraisers on the planet because poor people have to find a way to make something out of nothing. In order for them to survive, they very often do.

There were several nights growing up where my mom would purchase one large Jamaican dinner. It was a stew chicken, rice and peas, cabbage and plantain plate. That one plate would feed me, my brother and my sister first, then she would eat whatever was leftover. Now, one large Jamaican dinner is enough for one person to eat on their own. I look back on this experience fondly because it speaks to a couple of things. It speaks to her sacrifice, but it also spoke to her ability to make something out of nothing. It speaks to teamwork and being conscientious because I'm sure everybody in the house was hungry; but my brother, my sister and I had to be conscious of how much food we ate so that we each had something, but also so at the end my mom could eat from what we had leftover. That speaks to the innovation of somebody who's in a position of being poor or with limited resources. It's not something to be glorified for or aspire to. It was just my reality at the time, and had we been better prepared or empowered financially, perhaps I wouldn't have that story to tell you.

"Defeating Fear and Excuses."

Education, discipline, accountability, long-term planning, mentorship, and believing that you can do it. Those are the keys to defeating fear and excuses. Investing in yourself first through improving your mindset, reading, listening to audiobooks, podcast, lectures, going to events where you get that diversity of thought around how money is managed (by people who have money to manage), changing your environment, changing who you're around, controlling what you talk about, what kind of information you consume; all of these things are going to help overcome the tendency to make excuses and the fears that people have around money management.

My First Time Purchasing Stock

After opening a brokerage account and purchasing two shares of Apple, the first piece of advice I got on purchasing stock was: "Don't do it, it's too risky." This is when Apple was under 100 dollars a share, I was so excited. I was told that individual stocks are 'too risky" and that I should invest in mutual funds. Fortunately, that was not advice I took. I continued to purchase Apple stock over the years and have seen tremendous growth. (As of this writing, Apple is up over $200 a share inching towards $250!) Today I am a consistent and active investor in the market through various retirement vehicles and a few standalone applications on my phone. I've identified that you can build wealth through investing in the stock market and the reason why people lose money is because they are yielding to their emotions, to fear of risk, and to impulses to buy and sell trying to time the market. (Hint: you can't time the market!) People smile when they see the market climbing but start freaking out during the cycles of corrections. They call it "crashing" erroneously because the stock market doesn't crash, it corrects.

Going back to the example. If I would have taken the advice I was given, (which initially I did, actually. I didn't sell off my stock, but I did start looking at the mutual funds after that.) I would have decreased my earning potential in the stock market because I took advice blindly without understanding the amount of money I could have lost over time in management fees by investing in an actively managed mutual fund. I would, given the same dollar amount and same length of time in investing likely have lost more money investing in mutual funds than I would have invested in the stock.

One final thought I want to share about fear. I experience it REGULARLY and I do not want you to think otherwise. In fact, this last story I can laugh at now because of the education gained in hindsight, but it was the source of quiet embarrassment for a long time.

I finished reading a book on real estate and was invited to a local free seminar for people interested in getting started with real estate investing. At this free seminar, I was shown ways to invest in real estate with little money or no money and bad or no credit. At the end of the seminar, they hinted at the fact that I could potentially learn more at their follow up three-day seminar and that I would only have to pay $300 but that I could bring a free guest. It was recommended that the guest and I could split the $300 and only pay $150 a piece to get in. So I brought someone that I was mentoring, he was a little bit younger than I was and he wanted to learn more about real estate as well.

So we went for the three days, woke up very early to commute to the location and we were there from 8am until 6pm, learning about different strategies and techniques to invest in real estate. Every day for the three days, they hinted at this advanced training where I would learn even more secrets and have even more support and access to resources and materials that would make me be better able to essentially "retire" in a very short period of time. They were selling me a dream, and I was buying.

To add to their sales pitch, during this seminar they went over ways to "creatively finance" their advanced training. They discussed asking older relatives to access their IRAs or their 401ks and also included teaching us how to increase our credit limits so that we could tap into the cash advance portion of our line of credit to purchase the training. I was so convinced that fear actually worked in the opposite direction than it traditionally does. I was dealing with F.O.M.O. or the fear of missing out in this instance. I did not want to wonder "what if?" moving into the future. Remember that twelve-thousand dollars I told you I saved and lost? That's where I lost it.

The least expensive advanced training cost me $12,000. I tapped the entire savings. That was all the money I had, and it was the most money I had ever saved at one time. I purchased their training program because I did not ever want to think I allowed fear to stop me from building wealth. I learned a lot during the training; however, there was A LOT I could have learned for free on Google had I known where to look. But you don't know what you don't know, and I was not in a position at the time to execute on said strategies, so I kept it quiet except for sharing with a few trusted individuals. I worked through my embarrassment to recoup my savings. I was disenchanted with the idea of investing in myself afterwards because of my negative experience.

And so I share that story to illustrate a few things:

1. Don't let fear stop you from investing in yourself. Although I didn't get what I signed up for out of the training, I gained experience. I gained a special knowledge set that worked to my benefit later in life, and I dusted myself off and tried again.

2. Don't let F.O.M.O. or the fear of missing out be used as a tool to take advantage of your desperation. People in desperate conditions relating to their personal finance will often opt to find the latest "get rich quick" scheme over doing the work internally and externally because the sales pitch is so good it feels like you're being delivered a gift from above (re: "God will provide").

3. A lack of education caused me to buy at a premium what I could have consumed at a discount via Google and other books. Do your research and leverage resources. You can find a ton of "real estate guru's" on social media these days, each with a program crafted specially for someone naïve like you. Educate yourself first and then fill in the gaps.

4. Sometimes it's best to move in silence. I didn't tell anybody that I had the money. I didn't tell anybody that I spent that money. I could see the face my mom would have made in my head now. It was a learning experience I had to have on my own to get where I am today.

Having made what some would consider an irresponsible decision, in hindsight, I don't regret making that decision. I learned some valuable lessons and it inspired me (at a very high price point) to become even more consumed with educating myself financially. I recouped the money I had spent and accomplished my initial goal. So really that experience was a blessing in disguise because when they taught me how to raise my credit limit rapidly, I took those strategies and used them repeatedly overtime to get to the place I am now; not only do I have impeccable credit, but also higher than normal credit lines.

So yes, I know fear. I remember shaking as I was thinking about it. I remember calling maybe two or three people that night and asking them for their opinion on whether or not to pull the trigger. I remember one person in particular saying to me, "If anybody can make it happen, you can make happen." And that was all I needed to hear to make the decision that I was going to do it.

CHAPTER 5
YOU DON'T KNOW WHAT YOU DON'T KNOW: WHY HAVING A MENTOR IS IMPORTANT.

"Advice is free, experience you pay for."
—Baba Mwalimu R. Sabree I

OPRAH WINFREY ONCE SAID, "A mentor is someone who allows you to see the hope inside yourself." Mike Murdock said, "Mentorship is the key to extraordinary success." I say that a mentor is "someone you allow to have an influence over your thoughts, actions, and behaviors." I hope you let me be one of your mentors on this financial empowerment journey.

According to Oprah, a mentor brings HOPE. According to Mike Murdock, a mentor brings EXTRAORDINARY success. And I say, a mentor can be ANYONE. When reflecting on my personal financial journey my mentoring was not conventional.

For starters, I did not realize how important it was to have a mentor until I started learning about applying complex strategies. Stock picking, investing in the stock market, credit hacks, even some of the real estate investing strategies out there are examples of this. Many of these things you can learn through reading, but it's far easier to learn it by having someone show you or talk you through it with the wisdom of their experiences. Like my grandfather used to say, "Advice is free, experience you pay for."

Among many things, mentoring helps you navigate that fear factor we discussed earlier. It provides representation in that "if they can do it, I can do it too.". A mentor can also quell the anxieties that come with money management and losing money.

So why don't people get mentors?

Trust.

I've had people approach me about creating them a financial plan where I've actually turned them away because I wasn't sure I could help them. I've also had people approach me about creating them a financial plan and I've turned them away because I didn't believe they were serious about making change. How do you weed out the good ones from the bad? I establish a price point. Remember the discussion around "finding a way" to come up with money for things we don't need? I put people in a position to decide what's important to them. Are you soliciting my services because you want to make change or because you want me to do the work for you? What value do you place on my time? What value do I place on my time? Inversely, I'm sure the question running through your mind is what value will I provide? Is the investment worth it? There is certainly a reluctance to pay for consultative services, especially in so-called minority communities. The idea that "if it's not bleeding, broken, or dying" we don't have to visit the doctor or, let's use a free service instead of a paid one to "save" money, not realizing all the value we're leaving on the table without that consultative support. I'm the biggest advocate for independent learning on a subject; however, I'm also an advocate for paying someone to get it done right the first time. More on this later.

Due to that ingrained Scarcity Mindset it makes one reluctant to trust or want to pay for someone's services. There is certainly the need to make mention that professional services have taken advantage of poor and so-called minority people's lack of education—atrocities and documented cases of medical negligence that have occurred previously and continue to occur today (see Tuskegee Syphilis experiments). As a reaction to ingrained traumas and abuse we often opt to steer clear. We think about how there is never enough or that your resources are finite and thus you are not in a position to invest in additional information or resources to help you take things to the next level. This is another reason why representation matters. So what is the point of having a mentor then if you have to pay money to get one and it is not as easy as simply raising your hand and saying "I want a mentor?" How do we navigate issues of mistrust and trauma? Again, we self-educate.

Earlier, I told a story about walking into a car dealership and having the sales representative profile me. He made a decision in his mind about my ability to buy a car the moment I walked in. I had my typical New York get up on that day, too—Timberland boots, a Yankee fitted, a hoodie, and some jeans. Once he realized I had two-thousand in cash and a preapproval letter offering me an interest rate far below what he originally quoted me, his eyes bulged and he was determined to make his sale. What I didn't tell you was that when I decided to walk away based on my overall experience, the finance manager and the owner got involved and we started discussing my financial needs and preferences. I had a specific amount I wouldn't spend beyond and this car was outside of my budget by several thousand. He thought by giving me a one percent interest rate on a six year term I'd be impressed. It gets better, though. I told him that the reason I couldn't break my budget was because I was shopping for a house (my lender advised me not to exceed a certain dollar amount on financing or I'd compromise my application) to which the owner stated, "You don't need a house. A house isn't going to take you to and from work. That is a horrible investment" and looked back at the finance manager and started laughing at me. I asked him if he's ever bought a house, to which he replied smugly, "I own several." I left immediately and he called me every day with some new "deal" on that car for two weeks. I was young, I was inexperienced, and had I not had guidance from my lender, I likely would have been taken advantage of. (I needed a car at that moment, like yesterday...)

Get a Mentor on Your Financial Team

Is a paid mentor necessary for success? No, but allow me to share with you an example of why you might want to reconsider the idea of going through your financial journey without one. April 15th is Tax Day and usually from the day people get their W2 through the weeks leading up to that day you see swarms of people running to their nearest H&R Block or dusting off their free version of TurboTax. It's "floss" season where people start to think about the biggest size TV they can purchase, or what vacation they can go on with this tax refund. Some people go as far as to claim children that aren't theirs as dependents so they can get an even bigger return. Listen, I'm not here to judge anyone. While going to a pop-up shop that can do your taxes or using software like TurboTax to do taxes on your own is not a bad thing, is it the BEST?

I remember my first time paying a CPA to look at my taxes. Previously I was an avid user of the TurboTax software, but I had just started my first LLC and I wanted to get the business filing done accurately. Most people saw me as simply paying for the service, but I was also paying for a relationship. I had access to a professional and the expertise of that professional whenever I needed it. Throughout the course of the year he would advise me, share with me some highly effective strategies and help weigh in on key decisions I would make financially. His insights helped to decrease my tax liability while also giving me encouragement and recommendations around my financial goals and aspirations. This is the value of having a mentor.

A mentor helps to drive accountability. You are often forced to shift from a transactional mindset where it's one and done, to an ongoing relationship. This is vital to success because financial empowerment is not one and done. It's living and breathing, and you get out what you put in. "Accountability is the glue that ties commitment to results." Who doesn't want to see positive results with their finances? Having a mentor allows you to have that glue. That person who is able to help you in identifying trends, asking specific questions around what behaviors and tendencies you have to help you increase the likelihood of you succeeding.

Patience

That last reason many do not have a mentor is they don't have patience. The purpose of a mentor is to guide you. They're not there to do it for you. I've already discussed turning people I've deemed less than serious or committed away. I cannot emphasize enough that financial empowerment is a tedious process in some instances and requires time. It takes time to budget. It takes time to see a return. It takes time to break bad behaviors and establish new ones. A lot of people are looking to get rich quick or become one of those overnight success stories but getting out of a bad credit score or building up your savings from zero is not an overnight process, and it also requires you to trust in the process. I typically tell people it takes at least six months to see some serious positive movement with credit. Six months. That's almost the amount of time it takes for a baby to be born. If you can't commit to working on your financial goals with someone for at least six months, are you really serious about those goals?

Finding Mentors

Hopefully I've helped to remove some of the barriers in your mind to finding a mentor and you are ready to jump into the mentorship pool.

Here are some recommendations to where you can get a mentor to help with your relationship with money:

A professional in the field that can benefit you in terms of where you want to be long term. It's comparable to your relationship with your barber or hairdresser. They know you, you know them, and you know what to expect. Some examples include:

+ Tax Advisors
+ Real Estate Agents
+ Lenders
+ Financial Advisors

Now you might be wondering, would these people mentor you? My short answer is "you never know if you never ask." Lastly you can go to business owners and entrepreneurs. Often these are people who are independently wealthy who can lend their experience and expertise and share their story to help mentor you along with your journey. Again, you're not looking for someone to do it for you, you're looking for a blueprint to follow and someone to help hold you accountable.

If all else fails and you cannot find someone you can trust, you can always look to books, podcasts, YouTube videos, and Facebook groups as a starting point to help you get some information. While this is not as intimate as a relationship, the information there can still be helpful to you in getting your feet wet and on your way to achieving success with your finances. Some of the examples I like to pull from are Dave Ramsey, Grant Cardone, and Robert Kiyosaki. I don't necessarily agree with one hundred percent of their strategies, but I like to see what they talk about, what they are doing, and what approaches they've used to manage their finances and build wealth. Everyone is different. There is no cookie cutter approach to personal finance—just a lot of guru's and best practices. So take what you learn with a grain of salt and don't drink all the

Kool-Aid. Use these people as inspiration and guides of what could be and then go on to develop your own process that fits where you're at.

Bonus Tip: Networking Events/Associations

If I was guiding someone through the process of getting a mentor, I would definitely start by taking them to networking events where the subject matter or the common interest is around finances. Whether that be business development, entrepreneurship or specific to real estate investing, there are clubs and associations throughout the country where you can attend and start building relationships with people.

Here's a networking hack for those who are nervous about attending these events. What I find is that people LOVE to talk about themselves and their accomplishments. So long as you're able to, at least on a basic level, have a conversation, you can get tidbits of information and then continue to build a relationship over time that's mutually beneficial. Do not stop there, though. How many times do we go and collect business cards just to never use them again? Don't be a fishbowl, be a person. Engage with people. You can also create an event of your own. Introverted? No problem! Social media helps bring people together right from the comfort of their living room. Webinars, book clubs … there is literally no excuse. Multiple perspectives will help you to get a fuller scope of what is going on out there and how it can apply to you.

CHAPTER 6
LIVING PAYCHECK TO PAY-CHECK: DON'T LIVE BEYOND YOUR MEANS

"The men or women who drape themselves in gold and diamond necklaces and flaunt huge gaudy rings; who wear the most expensive shoes and clothes; as well as youth who dress in the most exclusive athletic wear or don designer handbags, wear a picture of wealth. In the absence of wealth's authenticity, they use these to paint a picture of success to avoid the embarrassment they believe they will experience if the world knew their true circumstances. The façade wears thin in the face of living paycheck to paycheck, renting instead of owning, following instead of leading, and struggling to just keep the lights on."

—Dr. Joy DeGruy

LIVING PAYCHECK TO PAYCHECK IS not a goal that one typically has when it comes to being financially responsible. In fact, many people would say that it is irresponsible to live that way, especially if you have the means to do otherwise. Fortunately, I'm in a position to do just that. That is, intentionally live paycheck to paycheck.

First let me say that this concept can certainly be met with offense and disgust by some, especially those who feel trapped in the cycle of living paycheck to paycheck involuntarily. It's definitely not something you think someone would brag about as an accomplishment or something they aspire for but bare with me as I dive into the strategic nature of this practice. My strategy in living paycheck to paycheck is to avoid giving myself lifestyle raises. Lifestyle raises typically occur when you get a pay increase and you find ways to spend that "extra" money instead of taking that money and saving it. My baseline for this strategy comes from the book, The Richest Man in Babylon, where the concept of taking ten percent of everything that you earn and putting it away for yourself over time and then having what it is you put away for yourself multiply, is introduced and is the foundation that frames my strategy.

When I get paid, I take ten percent out immediately before I look at anything else and move that into an account that doesn't get touched, NON-NEGOTIABLE. These are after-tax dollars meaning I've already paid into whatever pre-tax vehicles I invest in (HSA, 401k, etc.). Then I pay whatever debts or obligations I have in the following order of operations; things that will impact my credit first, whatever obligations I have that won't impact my credit second, and I'll leave myself enough money for living expenses to get me to the next pay period, but just enough that I don't go overboard. By structuring my finances in this way, I'm able to first of all, reduce my spending tremendously on things that are not going to add value or produce income, but also focus on my saving and investing. On top of that, something I do to really honor my commitment to this strategy is if I don't spend all the money I allocate toward living expenses by the time I get paid my next check, I actually start from zero again. So I'd take whatever was leftover, move that into my savings or investing account, and then from my new balance, start the process all over. Implementing this habit reinforces the discipline necessary to achieve financial success. I focus on saving and investing; however, the focus can easily be adapted to a debt elimination or business funding strategy. I know this seems a bit much or too strict, but in the spirit of being transparent, do know that I leave a little room for flexibility, but not much.

Living Within Your Means

You've probably heard the advice not to spend what you don't have, right? It's become embedded in the financial culture of our country to spend on credit as an extension of our income. However, living this way makes it nearly impossible to live within your means. Many people ask me about the idea of living within your means, especially when I speak to the various strategies I use. Here's my answer in regard to living within your means: I agree, when it applies to liabilities, that you should absolutely stay below your means, meaning things that are costing you money and/or are not putting money in your pocket.

(Liability= cost you money/Asset = makes you money)

However, when it comes to assets, I want to be able to control as much as I can for as little upfront capital as I can. I want to have as little "skin in the game" as possible. That's not to say that I or anyone else should overextend by purchasing assets (usually on credit) to the detriment of what your living expenses vs. your income is. So you definitely want to be able to cover at least your basic living expenses (including some wiggle room for saving/investing as mentioned above). A good example that demonstrates this is when someone is buying a house. Most people do not have enough upfront capital (cash) to be able to buy a house outright. Financing anything could be looked at as purchasing that is outside of your means. Student loans, car loans, houses, that computer from BestBuy that they offered you twenty percent off on if you applied for their credit card… etc. But is a house an asset? I think the answer will vary depending on who you ask. There are different benefits that can be leveraged from owning physical property that can in turn make you money, depending on your execution. Type of house, number of units, the way in which it was acquired, etc. are all angles where money can be made if executed from a place of education and awareness. Whatever your take, let's assume you do consider it an asset. What you most certainly want to ask yourself is: Are you able to make the monthly mortgage payments (mortgage+insurance+taxes in a lot of places), which now become part of your living expenses? I emphasize this because you may qualify for a larger loan (mortgage) than you can realistically afford. I'll get more into my experience with the home buying process later in the chapter called "leverage, leverage, leverage," but the point here is that you can, in certain instances "live beyond your means" to your benefit.

Besides living paycheck to paycheck, there are other things I do that some would consider financially irresponsible. One is I leverage credit, A LOT. The average American has three (as a rounded-up number) credit cards. I have three times that amount with a whopping total of nine credit cards. Not one, not two, not three, but nine. In addition to that, I typically have very close to zero cash savings, meaning I don't have any liquid savings. Most people are advised to have at least six months living expenses saved up as a safety net, I don't even have half of one. Irresponsible, right? You see I have enough credit across all of those cards to account for six months of emergency expenses if I really needed it and I can access them with relative ease. Emergencies (we hope) will occur few and far between, so rather than wait around on hope, I want my money (the ten percent plus that I save) to make me money with time. Now, this strategy won't work for everyone in every situation. This strategy may not even work for me tomorrow, six months, or a year from now! But the beauty in having the mindset and education around creating personalized financial strategies is that they can be adjusted and changed whenever your life changes.

I also don't always pay household bills on time. What I mean by that is I will sacrifice paying a bill that does not have a negative impact on my credit so that I can maintain the discipline I've established around paying myself first (see order of operations above). In the past I've let my internet bill, the electric bill, or even the gas bill go as far delinquent as getting a cutoff notice before I pay it because the money that I am ultimately able to put into an investment or savings account in advance of having that cutoff notice delivered is working to my benefit from a timing perspective. And then, when I realized that I absolutely must pay that bill, then of course I'll pay the bill. This requires a serious level of intimate awareness of your income and expenses. It's not something I recommend to others but it's worth noting for all of those people who say they live paycheck to paycheck and can't seem to save not even $25 a check.

Warning: I'm able to do this from the position of safety because:

A. I know I can push that limit.

B. I know I have the income coming in that will allow for me to pay that deferred payment in the long run.

If I didn't have the security in knowing I would be able to pay this month's bill three month from now, then, of course, there will be a priority of making sure that that bill gets paid immediately.

An added note on deferring bill payments and what types of bills this strategy applies to:

When I speak about deferring payments, I'm referring to my gas bill, my electric bill, my cell phone bill, and my internet or cable bill. You may be asking up to what point do I not pay the bill. The answer? To cut off or collections. This is something I'm sure many people in poverty are aware of. How much can you pay on this bill to keep it on just long enough to get to the next check? But there is definitely a delicate balance there. There are also late fees associated with paying the bill late. However, once I'm told that the bill's going to be cut off or once they let me know I'm in danger of the bill being sent to collections, I make sure I pay. I'm careful to make sure I'm able to pay in advance of that actually happening because the last thing I'd want is to defer payment of this bill for three months and now I have a total balance due that is much greater than I can afford to knock out in one payment and end up in a situation where I either get the cut off or have to deal with collections.

Tax Refunds

In the previous chapter, I talked about taxes and my relationship with my CPA. This is another area I've exercised "irresponsible" activity. While many get excited about tax season because they've got their hearts set on that new TV or vacation package, I do not look forward to this. What most people don't understand when it comes to getting a refund is that they've been overpaying the government throughout the course of the year and that the money you're getting back is actually your own money which the government has been holding on to interest free for the entire year. Let me repeat that, you're essentially giving a loan to the government INTEREST FREE. This means you're actually losing money or rather losing value on the money you were not getting out of your check because it's not doing anything (imagine purchasing a security that produced dividends four times a year with the money you overpay the government every year).

What do I do? I pay less in taxes throughout the year by manipulating my withholding values so that I have as close to a zero refund as possible without owing while increasing the amount of money in my paycheck each pay period. I couple this with the depreciation of assets that I own, itemized deductions, and business expenses. This is something that an accountant or a CPA would be consulted around in terms of the deployment of this strategy. It's worth noting that a major component to building wealth is understanding that it's not how much you make, but how much you keep that matters. Someone could be making a six-figure salary and only keeping half of it after taxes, while someone making $50,000 salary keeps the majority of it because they understand the manipulation of taxes.

Try to think differently now when you get your refund about how you allocate it. Do you really need a new TV? Can you use that toward starting an investment or retirement account? Maybe you want to work toward purchasing real estate. You've lost a year's worth of use with that money; it's time to get it circulated again in a way that going to make you money. If all else fails invest in yourself, you are your greatest asset. Take a course, buy a few books, go to a conference, build relationships. You can save for that vacation throughout the year.

401k

I recently posted a Twitter thread that started with "I stopped contributing to my company sponsored 401(k) and here's why."

People.

Went.

Crazy!

How dare I bash the holy grail of retirement planning!? In some conversations I've referred to it as people's "save me" fund. "My company matches me dollar for dollar! Not contributing is leaving money on the table!" [Insert the regurgitation of what you're force fed about planning for retirement.] This is huge because people are taught to blindly get a "good" job with a 401k and save as much as you can for retirement. So that's what they do without having even a basic understanding of the funds that are being offered within the company plan or the expenses of managing those funds that come out of your overall return.

I leverage the 401k definitely as an investing and saving vehicle, but not a vehicle for long term retirement planning. I think that if a company is offering a match, sure that's free money to an extent. So the general rule of thumb is that whatever the company matches up to is what you want to contribute up to.

However, what I've done in discontinuing my contributions to the 401k is taking sole control of my retirement planning via, retirement vehicles such as the Roth IRA and HSA making contributions on my own deliberately across a much wider range of fund or equity investments (stocks). Being able to invest that money in what I choose to invest that money in eliminates management fees and expenses because I'm actually performing the management myself and keeping those fees and expenses in my pocket while continuing to invest into that long term retirement vehicle. I've certainly leveraged the 401k for its benefits, and I've contributed to them for longer terms as well. In no way am I discouraging others from contributing. I'm simply shedding light on something that isn't well known. Contributing to that 401k (or not contributing) is definitely going to move the dial on how much you take home, thus impacting or enhancing your ability to live "paycheck to paycheck."

Results of Living "Financially Irresponsible"

Before I dive into the benefits of the strategies I use, I want to highlight the fact that my approach is definitely high risk by a lot of standards and certainly "irresponsible" by a set of others. I'm at a place in my life where I can comfortably take those kinds of risks and make risky decisions with relative ease. I also don't have anyone depending on me. I'm able to play around with different strategies I've learned about from the research I've done and the education I've acquired over time. It does require that I have laser focus and a strong discipline, but it allows for me to manage my income, my debt, my saving, and my investing on my own terms.

Whereas security is certainly a priority for a lot of people who are not as financially empowered or informed, I have the freedom to control a lot of those factors in a way most people can't or most won't because they're afraid of what that ultimately can spell for them in terms of a disaster. Whether that be losing control of their debt, not having enough income, not establishing savings or not even entertaining the idea of investing, I really get to hold those elements in the palm of my hand and determine the direction and the flow of those decisions. My hope is that after reading this book you will, too. A lot of it is trial and error and while I could be doing it to a greater capacity, I draw a great satisfaction from being able to A) speak to the fact that I have that kind of control and B) certainly not having to blindly relinquish control of those factors to somebody else.

Lastly, I'm able to pay it forward (more on this in the final chapter of the book), taking what I've learned through a variety of different sources, both active and passive learning, and share it with other people. This gives my life more purpose and gives me a place to share and add value to other people who may not have the same kind of clarity I do.

So, I started this chapter explaining how and why I live paycheck to paycheck, but I hope the illustrations drawn throughout not only inspire you to stop living paycheck to paycheck if you're doing so involuntarily and start living paycheck to paycheck on your terms.

PART 2

THE FIRST PART OF THIS book covered a lot of the mental and spiritual components to mastering your money. Ultimately, we discussed the need to work from within; addressing the fears, myths, and, dare I say, superstitious tendencies common to the un-empowered. The next part of this book is going to be a more in-depth introduction to financial terms, products, and high level of strategy coming from my own experiences, observations, and research. It should be noted that my approach to financial education is not one size fits all. I look at as many pieces as I can to understand how to connect them in a way that is advantageous to the end user. That said, different people's circumstances and where they are in life, their mindset, and the means by which they make money is definitely going to influence some of what my guidance entails. The last time for the readers who have conveniently skipped all previous iterations of my disclosure:

This is not to be taken as advice. This is intended to serve as inspiration and a catalyst for a deeper dive into financial education. This book's contents are a summary of my personal experiences and personal disciplines. Adopt them at your own risk. Finally, if you're interested in having me come speak to a group, facilitate a workshop, or participate on a panel, feel free to visit my website or reach out to me via social media at **www.RahkimSabree.com**.

I have mentored and assisted individuals and groups on many of the subjects this book covers. I highly suggest and encourage that as a supplement to the topics and the terms I introduce, that the readers continue their education by expounding on the framework and baseline terminologies I provide.

At the end of this book, you'll find a glossary with terms I've hand selected so you can quickly and easily identify and apply them to your financial vocabulary.

What's the difference between a savings account and a money market account? What are the different types of retirement vehicles? What is an asset? How do I save and budget? What's the difference between a credit report and a credit score and what are the factors that make up both? What's leverage? All of these questions and more will be addressed.

I want you to know that you are the master of your fate. The information in this book does not take away ownership and accountability from you as the reader to continue your education, challenge what you've read, and bring it into different circles to start the conversation.

Are you ready? Let's dive into the rest of the book, I cannot

wait to share with you what this journey has taught me
and hear how it benefits you.

CHAPTER 7
PAY YOURSELF FIRST

"A part of all you earn is yours to keep."
—George S. Clason, *The Richest Man in Babylon*

In part one of the book, we talked about the concept of paying yourself first, but I felt that a specific section should be devoted to this as it serves as the base for a lot of the principles I employ on my personal wealth building journey.

"Pay yourself first" is almost a mantra in the personal finance space that speaks to the practice of making sure you put money aside for you before spending or paying any debt. It's a two-fold discipline that pushes one to budget (or create a system of income estimation and allocation) and save (or stash money away toward a specific purpose or goal) in order to build wealth.

From a young age, I've always been taught the value of saving. My grandfather introduced me to this 1/3 theory of sorts where he said I should spend a third, save a third, and invest a third. I didn't really understand the concept of investing or how I could do it at such a young age, but

I did make a conscious effort to save at least a portion of what I got. How long I saved, well that's a different story.

However, it's hard to save when you have nothing left to save from; do I have a witness? As a child I didn't have living expenses because I was cared for. However, today, like many of you, I have to balance feeding and clothing myself, keeping a roof over my head, keeping the lights on, etc.

In books like, Rich Dad, Poor Dad or The Richest Man in Babylon paying yourself first is a theme and focal point as the initial building block to a larger wealth building strategy. When I was initially exposed to these books, it changed the way I looked at my income, from trying to save what's left to prioritizing saving for me first and spending what's left. I typically maintain a target of ten to twenty percent of my income between various savings and investing vehicles BEFORE I can think to touch it. Start today and find a number percentage you're comfortable with. Is it five, ten, fifteen, twenty percent? Do the math and figure it out today, you'll thank me later.

When you examine the average worker, there's an emphasis on paying taxes, paying our bills, and trying to survive on what's left. So the idea of paying ourselves first is foreign, but it does have its benefits. I like to think about it as a non-negotiable bill due to me. Why should the government and other bill collectors get my hard-earned dollars before I do? Why can't a bill be late because I ran out of money after paying myself first, opposed to missing an opportunity to fund my savings because I paid all my bills on time. To be clear, I'm not advocating for you to not pay your bills on time or at all. That would truly be irresponsible of both of us, but I am speaking to the VALUE we place on ourselves as a result of being financially empowered. Paying ourselves first benefits us by putting us in a position to grow our saving and investing ability over time, which in turn should put us in a position to generate additional income. We should be spending our money on things that in turn have the potential to make us more money. Making money just to pay bills and survive won't do that for us.

One of the strategies I use in addressing this is understanding which bills I can avoid paying on time with minimal consequences, and which bills I absolutely need to pay in order to maintain good credit standing. I discuss this in part one of this book with deferred payment strategies in the chapter "Living Paycheck to Paycheck." I'm even aware that credit bills can be up to twenty-nine days late without having a negative reporting show up on my credit report (that doesn't mean I won't get hit with a late fee though!). Again, for me, bill priority is established first by what is reportable to the credit bureaus and then by what supports my household. Examples of this include my phone bill, gas bill, power bill, and things of that sort as shared earlier.

Saving Best Practices

While we all should know the basics of saving, we often have a hard time doing it. It doesn't help that there are a barrage of savings vehicles and platforms to choose from. Here are some factors to consider when making the decision.

First, the savings vehicle. A good question to ask yourself

is why are you saving? What's it for? Are you saving just because you were taught to do so? Trying to buy a car? Looking to put a down payment on a house? Believe it or not, your short- or long-term goals will dictate where you house your savings. Second, how often would you need access to that money. This would be determined by your answer to the previous question. Third, the concept of inflation, which is the decrease in purchasing power of money in relation to the increase in the price of goods and services. The last point is especially relevant for those who believe a good way to manage their savings is by having a stockpile of money in a shoe box or under the mattress. We discussed inflation earlier but if your savings goal is retirement then this method is actually costing you as time moves on.

One feature of a lot of savings vehicles you can use to help with savings is Automation.

Automation of savings absolutely makes saving easier because you're not thinking about having to take that conscious action. For example, I calculate what is ten percent of my take home pay and I have that money automatically direct deposited into a separate account that I then move into a brokerage account. If you have a 401k or 403b you're likely familiar with this concept because the money comes out before you can miss it.

Some other strategies that I've used in the past include having bank accounts at multiple banks. I typically make it much more difficult or inconvenient for me to access money held with a bank that is not my primary; whether it be by not having an ATM card attached to it, or having it geographically out of the way so that if I was to ever get tempted to go there I would actually have to plan that trip and really work to make that happen.

I've also increased my withholding from a tax perspective so that at the end of the year I get a larger refund. This is in contradiction to the more recent strategy I employ around decreasing my withholding because my overpayment over the course of the year is not growing my money and thus it is not serving to my benefit until I get it in that one lump sum after filing. So for maybe the newbie to saving and saving strategy, that might be a good starting point. But ultimately you want to get to a point where you're in full control of what happens to your income and that you're consciously deciding based off established disciplines and intentional actions to move that money into a savings or an investment vehicle.

So now that you are aware of a few strategies, pick a type of savings account that is not riddled with fees and start to save. Remember the purpose of the savings account is indeed to save. You should not be regularly accessing that money, if ever at all. I like to save to invest. The following are some different ideas around investing so that the money gets put to work.

Stocks

When people think about wealth, the term stocks often comes up. For the sake of our conversation stocks are just a representation of ownership in a company. A common question I get from people who are wanting to get into the financial space and control their money is "which stocks should I invest in?"

The best answer I can give is that you should do careful research not just into stocks but overall investing strategies. Looking into what vehicle to use, what benefits tax wise it affords you or the disadvantage of it, these are factors to consider before you even start buying stocks. It's also important to think long-term and not in the mindset of "get rich quick." This is not me saying that one should not invest in stocks. I firmly believe it's irresponsible not to explore how you can use that vehicle and others to help you build wealth.

When it comes to getting started with investing in the stock market, the one book that is frequently referred to is The Intelligent Investor by Benjamin Graham. Warren Buffet, a man regarded as a master stock picker and investor, studied that book himself and describes it as having changed his life! Buffet is known to frequently give advice to passive investors to look at low cost index funds, which are basically a group of stocks and other securities in a mutual fund that have a low management fee and follow a particular index. Those indexes can follow real estate, commodities, the S&P 500, or the Dow Jones Industrial Average. A lot of times people who are newer to investing in the stock market start with index funds or ETFs which are electronically traded funds, (basically a bag of different stocks that give you access to diversity or diversification while still allowing you to play the stock market game).

A lot of people also look at individual stocks that they like. I would not give specific investing advice in terms of what stocks to purchase, but I would recommend that people looking into investing in the stock market look at stocks of companies whose products you use every day. One favorite stock of mine is Apple. I'm a big fan of Apple products. I have an iPhone, the Apple Watch, a MacBook, and several iPads. So, because I really like Apple, and I really know about Apple, I like to buy them. But remember, there's a difference between investing for the long term or trying to time the market. You'll hear many professionals say, "You can't time the market."

My personal approach to investing in stock is to buy for the long haul. So when I look at the stock market and stock market purchases, I'll look at locking in for ten-year increments, rather than day to day, month to month, or even year to year. A lot of times where people lose in the stock market is with their emotions and seeing the ups and downs of the value of the stock. Instead of looking at consistent contributions to the purchase of either the same stock or the same group of stocks over time, especially if those stocks are paying you as an owner dividend, which is a form of passive income. So my advice for those getting in the stock market is get in for the long haul and invest in things you know.

If stocks are not your thing, there are other forms of investing available.

Investments Besides Stocks

You can buy a business, buy equity into a business, or start a business of your own. You can become an early investor and help somebody else get their business off the ground. Investing in real estate, which is a favorite topic of mine, investing in commodities such as gold, oil, silver, investing in crypto currency, and even Forex are just some examples of things you can invest in.

But what about education? A lot of time when people think about investing, they don't think about investing in education as a means to building wealth. That education creates a platform, or foundation for you to build off from a place of confidence and knowledge that will get you into the arenas of all the different investing strategies we talked about. Investing in education will teach you how to invest in real estate, how to invest in the stock market, about the crypto currencies and buying into businesses. It's like the story I told earlier about investing into that real estate training program I didn't have the best experience with. I couldn't get past the amount I spent versus what was promised in the sales pitch, but it was truly an investment in my education because what I walked away with wasn't an immediate monetary gain that I could measure, but it was knowledge and it was confidence in being able to navigate some investing strategies for real estate specifically. It also taught me the power of networking and interacting with other people. I was able to understand how to improve my credit, understand where people are in terms of wealth building strategies that they employ and understanding how to create a business entity. In a way, that was the greatest benefit for me.

Budgeting

People look at budgeting kind of like putting themselves on some sort of financial diet. The issue with this is we know fad diets don't last long. I'd recommend changing your approach to budgeting as a lifestyle change rather than a diet.

When you budget, you're factoring in your income, what your expected and unexpected expenses are, and how much you can allocate toward savings in such a way that your discipline is not compromised over a period of however long you're looking to save (hopefully always!). And, of course, we're talking about saving to build wealth, so the saving component of your budgeting is really for long-term growth. It's necessary to understand the flow of your income and expenses through budgeting so that you can better determine where your money goes and how much of your money stays with you. So failing to plan is planning to fail. When you don't budget, you're failing to plan, which ultimately puts you in a position to end up with zero at the end of the day. And lastly, without budgeting, we learn to rely on credit as an extension of income, which puts us into debt. So rather than building wealth, we're actually digging a hole further away from it.

So remember, a portion of everything you earn is yours. Make it a priority to guard that, pay YOU first as the non-negotiable bill and watch how quickly your money grows.

CHAPTER 8
THE CREDIT GAME AND BECOMING CREDIT CONSCIOUS

"An 800-credit score has more purchasing power than $100K."

—Unknown

Credit Consciousness

WHAT DOES IT MEAN TO be credit conscious? I use the term credit conscious to describe a turning point for me when I realized what credit was and how it impacted my life (and would impact) my future. Being credit conscious means understanding credit, the factors that contribute toward good or bad credit and knowing how to manage credit. I made reference earlier to the priority in which I pay my bills, based on what is reportable and what I can defer. This is a result of being credit conscious.

I started using the term when I had to explain credit and when I became aware of credit. Many people know that credit exists and know what credit is, but they don't understand how it works, or how it impacts them. It's true that people navigate in a world influenced by credit worthiness without ever establishing credit. There are also people who abuse credit and don't fully understand how important it is to maintain. I've certainly seen cases where people will get a credit card, use it, and pay it when they feel like it or won't pay it at all. Eventually this results in the account going to collections. That now becomes a negative item that stains their credit report for at least seven years.

Credit, A Necessity?

I advised a couple once who had trouble budgeting. They were trying to save to buy a house but also pay down an auto loan on a truck. The husband had bad credit and was paying nineteen percent interest on the truck! The couple was frustrated because of his credit and wanted an immediate fix. They were torn between saving for the purpose of purchasing a home or paying off the truck. My advice to them was that they should aggressively pay off the truck. They took that advice and started budgeting toward saving large chunks of money. They took the money they had already saved and applied it to paying down the truck and then paid extra until the truck was paid off. Eventually, they very rapidly recouped and exceeded their initial savings. They improved their credit situation collectively and were on their way to initiate the home buying process. Later, they thanked me as they didn't initially realize how great a strain the husband's bad credit was on the household finances. Don't let this be you.

I've witnessed people be turned down from jobs because of their credit. I've even seen people who have higher rates on their insurance because of their credit, or people denied residence who were not approved because of their credit. So when people truly understand the significance that credit plays, they'll pay more attention to it, and be much more vigilant in their practices around managing and protecting that credit. Remember that story about me walking into the car dealership and being profiled? Before going I got a preapproval letter for an auto loan through my bank which locked me in at an interest rate somewhere in the area of three percent. I had a huge bargaining chip in my pocket when I sat down with the sales rep. At no point could he bully me based on his internal biases of my age, race, or otherwise, because I already secured funding irrespective of all of that. He HAD to play by my rules regarding rates which is why he called over the owner. I had great credit and if they wanted me to finance through them, they would have to beat my rate. That was empowering to me.

The Good Credit Trap

Something I've seen people fall into all the time is having good credit and co-signing for somebody who's not accountable or doesn't honor their commitment to paying debt. I NEVER, and I mean never, recommend anyone co-signing on a loan for someone if that loan doesn't serve their interest. I've heard cases where Grandma co-signs her grandson's student loans and he never pays so she gets stuck with the obligation, lest her credit be destroyed. It's just not worth it because you ultimately assume responsibility for the loan. As a consequence, the person's once good credit is now rolling, because of someone else's irresponsibility in paying their obligation. This, however, can be leveraged in reverse to build someone's credit. When my younger sister was seventeen, I added her as an authorized user on one of my credit cards. She never got the card, but she benefited from my limit and payment history. When she turned eighteen, she had a "head start" and was able to take out credit accounts of her own with no problem. In this scenario, I was careful to control all the variables. I educated her on best practices of using credit cards, and I kept the card from her. As an authorized user, she could make purchases but was not obligated to pay them back. That would be on me.

Building A Credit Score

When I first started writing this book, I was proud (but resistant) to display the badge of honor many seek in the world of credit building—my 800 credit score. How I did it, alone, has been the subject of many conversations how I did it. I'll get into my credit story in a second, but first, I want to spend some time on a term I'm sure you have heard before and that is FICO. FICO stands for the Fair Isaac Corporation. FICO is the first company to offer a credit risk model with a score. In the credit world, there are many credit scoring models. However, the most widely known and accepted is FICO. Within that scoring method, scores can range from 300 to 850. The factors that make up your credit score include payment history, length of credit history, number of accounts, credit mix, utilization, and number of hard inquiries.

> *"Understanding how the credit model works, and where you stand within this model, is the first step to becoming credit conscious."*
>
> —RAHKIM SABREE

My Credit Story

When I was twenty-one, I started working at a bank and some of the benefits associated with working at that bank included having fee waived accounts and discounted interest rates on a credit card.

Up to that point I had previously applied for multiple credit cards at different department stores like Macy's, Express, and Sears, to name a few. Somewhere along the line someone shared with me this myth that the best starter cards for people with no credit are retail store cards. This is a myth. Every store card I applied for I got denied. I didn't know anything about credit, so I was always sold on that twenty percent discount on my first purchase. Having been denied every time previously, when I was asked if I wanted to apply for this bank card, I was pretty sure that that I would get denied as well. After thinking about it, I said why not, let's go for it. So when I got approved, the credit card credit limit was 300 dollars and I was ecstatic.

When I got the approval letter, the bank offered to send me a free copy of my credit report. The approval letter displayed what my credit score was and told me what factors led into the decision-making process, which included delinquencies on my student loans. While I was aware that I had student loans and I had to pay those loans, I didn't realize not paying them would negatively impact my credit. So I didn't pay them. What eventually ended up happening was my student loans went delinquent up to 120 days. That resulted in me having four different negative remarks on my two different loan accounts.

Correcting Credit

That negative comment on my credit report was visible every time I applied for credit and came up for any lender who was looking to pull credit on my behalf. Credit cards, personal loans, car loans, insurance, employment, anything that requires getting my credit report. The first course of action for me after becoming credit conscious was to make sure that my loans got current.

I became obsessed with understanding credit and how to improve it. I often heard peers discuss their high credit scores or how they've had a credit card since they were sixteen years old. I needed to aggressively build my credit so the second course of action for me was to navigate around those negative marks on my credit report and build my credit to the point where those marks almost didn't matter anymore. I was successful over a period of nearly ten long disciplined and experimental years. That same $300 credit card I was approved for on a whim commands well over a $30,000 limit now.

"Understanding those factors that make up your FICO score and working within that understanding to improve your standings from a rating perspective is a key. The benefit of improving your standings is that when a lender is assessing risk, they can extend you more credit or additional lines of credit."

—Rahkim Sabree

Having Multiple Credit Lines

I originally understood that a credit mix was important, and I knew I needed more than one line of credit. Eventually, I had gotten to a point where I had over five credit cards and understood that credit cards or a revolving line of credit was only one piece to the credit mix, and I needed some installment loans. An installment loan is a loan for a lump sum paid over a number of payments. Car loans, mortgages, personal loans, and student loans are all installment loans.

I secured my first installment loan by visiting a local Credit Union. I put down $2,000 as collateral on a personal loan for the same amount. From there, I simply used the proceeds of the loan to pay back the loan. Now I had a positive history of installment payments over the course of the year. Since the payment history was greater than six months and I had paid back the installment loan, my credit score improved. Beyond that, I took out another installment loan, for the purchase of a used car I already had the cash to purchase. I financed the car and paid off the financing for it over time with the money I had saved to pay off the car. In this way, I was not putting myself in a situation where I could lose, because I already had the money to pay it off. At the end of the day, I paid more money in both instances than what was given to me when factoring in interest but today I have access to much more credit as a result of paying that small interest.

In addition to those varied credit cards and installment loans I had on my credit report, I managed the revolving debt quite well. I typically keep all of my credit cards with less than thirty percent utilization. I was pretty adamant about making sure my card balances didn't go above thirty percent of what the total limit was. So, if I knew that I needed to use more of the credit, I also knew that I needed to increase the total amount of credit I had at my disposal.

So if you're looking at $300 limit, then thirty percent utilization is $100. If you're looking at a $10,000 limit, you know that a thirty percent utilization is $3,000.

Credit Limits

I made a regular practice of asking for credit line increases every six months to a year or two. I was also very strategic about credit inquiry pools, so I didn't apply for credit outside of a defined and strategic plan. I knew that credit inquiries stayed on your credit report for up to two years. So I timed my inquiries to fall off around the same time, two years into the future, so I knew that at this particular point in time I would have this number of inquiries showing up on my credit report. I factored in things like credit history and I knew that no matter what, I had to keep the oldest credit card I had open and active, because my credit history was so new that I needed to have patience and wait. I also understood that every time I opened up a new credit account, it shortened the length of my average credit history because that new account is factored into the average. So after a while I stopped opening accounts and just focused on increasing my credit limits and keeping my utilization low.

Monitoring Credit

Lastly, I also monitor my credit report and my credit score regularly. There's a myth circulated that doing so hurts your credit. This is a myth. Regular hard credit pulls hurt your credit. There are a variety of ways to check your credit report and score without doing a hard pull.

Did you know that you get one free copy of your credit report from each one of the credit bureaus (Experian, Equifax, and Transunion) per year? If you visit AnnualCreditReport.com you can select to pull one report or all three at the same time. Every year I would pull all three credit reports or stagger each credit throughout the course of the year so I could make sure there was nothing showing up on my credit report that either wasn't mine or wasn't accurate.

On that note, there are too many instances of young people coming of age to realize some bill or obligation has been placed in their name and thus negatively impacts their credit. This is fraud, don't do it.

All of those factors, practices, and disciplines around managing the credit I had while acquiring new lines of credit, taking the hit around interest payments, practicing strategic timing for when I allowed my credit to be pulled, and an almost obsessive learning style, allowed me to grow in my credit worthiness. Combined, these factors landed me in a place where my credit reached the 800s.

The Badge, Striving for an 800 Credit Score

Is an 800-credit score important to have? To be honest, not really. However, it's definitely an attainable and sought-after goal.

> "In my eyes, an 800-credit score is an eventuality, but the goal should really be to focus on getting to a level of excellent credit, which would be the higher end of the 700s."
>
> —RAHKIM SABREE

Breaking 800 is certainly a badge of honor for someone who didn't understand credit and formerly had multiple delinquencies. However, the goal shouldn't be placed more on a numeric representation of your credit worthiness than on your focus to demonstrate that you can manage credit effectively. Sure, you'll be privy to premium rates, special card offers, and incentives most people don't get access to, but that's it. So, it was not a goal of mine in the process of building credit to get an 800 credit score per se. My goal was to get my credit to a point and place where in managing my credit—whether it be the lines of credit I had access to, or in the application for additional lines of credit—I was not going to be turned away. Having credit in the high 700s is definitely considered an achievement. Having that is going to land you many of the same, if not exactly the same rates and opportunities that an 800-credit score or higher is going to. These numbers fluctuate as you navigate and leverage the credit landscape.

I think a lot of people get hung up on the numeric score in the same way that people get hung up on budgeting. It's not a diet, it's a lifestyle and people should really be focusing their attention on the DISCIPLINE and the PRACTICE.

> "As long as you're maintaining the discipline and incorporating best practices into your financial lifestyle, then your credit score or budgeting practices are going to be solid, which will serve the purpose you're looking for them to serve."
>
> —RAHKIM SABREE

Budget Masters

It's important to remember that the same people who are masters at budgeting are not looking to necessarily attain anything specific numerically. They have the end goal of being able to provide more value toward whatever their goal or dream is, whether that be long-term wealth building or even vacation. They're not looking at it as a short-term sprint, accomplish their goal, and then fall back into old ways. They're looking to make a lifestyle change so that they can do the things that matter to them.

The 800 Club

At present the 800-credit score hasn't afforded me anything besides bragging rights. If I'm going to be honest, I haven't really leveraged my score yet because I haven't needed to. I have all the credit lines I could use at the moment. I purchased my house, have a brand new car, and the interest rates on everything that I'm being charged are low. So outside of what it could do for me in terms of giving me access to maybe more capital, it's given me confidence and authority of knowing I could demand the best of what I'm looking for without much fuss and being able to impart my experience on people like you.

For me, having and maintaining the 800-credit score is important for when I need to use it. So let's say I decide that there's a business opportunity I want to take advantage of and need some startup capital for. I know I have that score in my arsenal of things to leverage.

The credit game, as I like to refer to it, is taking in credit consciousness and applying it to work in your best interest. Whether that'd be helping someone build their own credit or taking advantage of low interest rates and extensions of credit to fund lucrative business goals. It could mean applying leverage and using very little of yours and a lot of someone else's to control a larger asset.

Playing the Credit Game

I will say this, playing with other people's money (OPM) is fun but can get dangerous quickly, especially when interest is added. I'm a big fan of the balance transfer offer that a lot of credit cards provide in that they give you zero percent interest on purchases and balance transfers for twelve to fifteen months. I think the highest I've seen is eighteen months at zero percent. So all you're paying is principle, and no interest for that period of time.

In the past I've taken the convenience check associated with that card offer and cashed it for a specified amount into my checking account. A convenience check is a check where you can write on the credit limit that you have access to. I took a convenience check on a credit card that was offering me zero percent for a year and wrote a check to myself that I then cashed. I used that cash to pay off high interest debt so that I can then focus on knocking down only principal payments.

The Game of Credit and Mistakes

What are ways people play the credit game wrong?

Way #1: One is by ignoring credit. Some people refuse to establish or take out credit based on internalized trauma or fears that come from other people. They lose the game because they're not playing.

Way #2: Having a credit card but not implementing the strategy around increasing your credit limit to accommodate your credit usage. Let's say you have a $3,000 credit card limit and you need to make a purchase for $2,000. Yes, you have access to a credit line that allows you to make that purchase, but you're now using two thirds of your available credit. If you don't pay that balance off immediately (or most of it by the time the statement cycle closes), then you're stuck with a high utilization over thirty percent.

Way #3: Abusing credit. Using credit as an extension of your income or using credit to purchase things of no value or low value is not going to make you money. It creates liability, meaning you get stuck with the debt that now forces you budget more of your available income toward paying that debt down, and away from saving and investing. There's definitely a difference between having credit and managing it. If you've abused credit in the past and you're trying to get out of debt, the next page refers to Dave Ramey's "Debt Snowball" method which I'd like to mention.

How to get out of Debt using a Debt Snowball

(found on DaveRamsey.com)

1. List your debts in order from smallest total payoff balance to the largest.

Don't worry about the interest rate, unless two of the debts have a similar payoff balance. In that case, pay off the one with the highest interest rate first.

Debts	Total Payoff	Min. Payment
Credit Card 1	$100	$25
Hospital Bill	$1,000	$250
Home Depot	$5,000	$175
Total	$6,100	$450

2. Get your debt snowball rolling by paying as much as you can on the smallest balance.

Only make minimum payments on all the other debts and put everything you can into the first debt. When you knock one out, cross it off. This will show you how close you are to becoming debt-free and help keep you fired up!

3. Once you've paid something off, move on to the next debt on the list.

As the payments roll over, watch how fast your payoffs grow. You can be out of debt sooner than you think.

CHAPTER 9
LEVERAGE, LEVERAGE, LEVERAGE

THERE IS WORKING HARDER AND there's working smarter. This is how leverage comes into to play to help you reach your financial goals.

Debt vs. Debt-Free

There are different schools of thought when it comes to debt. Being a student of money and personal finance, I like to pull from different thought leaders in the field of financial education. There's a lot of commentary on whether or not you should be debt free, completely debt free, or if you should "go as far into debt as humanly possible." What I mean by that is that there is good debt and bad debt. When most people hear the word debt, they associate it with a negative connotation because there's so many stories relating to people who are under tremendous amounts of bad debt.

But let's talk about good debt. A lot of people, especially in the world of real estate, rely on debt to build wealth.

Good debt is debt that you take out on something that is producing income for you or making money.

A multifamily (or two plus unit residential property) can serve as something that's going to be income producing. That would turn any mortgage on the property to good debt because it's debt for something that is ultimately going to be producing income.

Consumer Debt

Consumer debt, or as it's referred most frequently to credit card debt, can be applied to any debt used for consumption and not investment or doing business. Consumer debt is what you would consider bad debt.

So back to leverage; leverage is being able to use other people's money (OPM) to help in the acquisition or control of an income producing asset. You can either take advantage of traditional financing, which most frequently would be your bank, or you can take advantage of non-traditional financing. Non-traditional financing involves taking advantage of other ways that allow you to use money that's not yours to help in the acquisition and control of an asset. Credit cards and personal loans have been used to create good debt; however, let's say you and a group of friends decide to start a business and you all take a cash advance out on your credit cards. Let's say you can take $2000 a piece, split up among five people. That's $10,000 you have collectively to put a down payment on or purchase a business or asset that's going to make you enough money to pay off all the debt across the group, but then allow for you to continue to draw income in the future.

Purchasing real estate is the most intimate example of leverage to me. When I bought my house, I took advantage of the FHA loan which required that I put down only 3.5 percent of the purchase price of the property. I had negotiated that the seller would pay the closing cost and I showed up to the closing table with a cashier's check for the amount of my down payment. But the money used to purchase that check was not my own. I was able to use my credit card to cover my down payment, leveraging the bank's money two times. First with the mortgage and second with the credit to fund the purchase or acquisition of an item that is income producing to me. Of course, eventually I had to pay that money back and make mortgage payments, but I essentially purchased a property with little to no money of my own at closing.

Quickly, on the topic of home ownership, I backed into my strategy of buying a multifamily property for the income benefits. I found a deal in a neighborhood that is appreciating, and I was able to get my hands on a property that was part of an estate, so it was lower than the appraised value of the house. This series of events may not happen for you, or may not be your ultimate goal in homeownership but I'm writing this, however, to encourage you to explore your options around home ownership and the various programs offered to help with down payment assistance, or low down payments like FHA. I once didn't think it was even in the cards for me to own a home before thirty but it's doable, you just have to educate yourself.

CHAPTER 10
LONG-TERM PLANNING AND LONG-TERM DISCIPLINE

"Compound interest is the eighth wonder of the world. He who understands it, earns it ... he who doesn't ... pays it."

WHERE DO PEOPLE GO WRONG when it comes to planning? In failing to plan. That sounds really simple, but it's not. Benjamin Franklin is often credited with saying, "Failing to plan is planning to fail." I think that can especially be applied when it comes to planning for wealth building and retirement, because those take time.

> "The lack of planning is where people go wrong, because people feel as if they can always do it tomorrow."
>
> —RAHKIM SABREE

The quote I open this chapter with is often credited to Albert Einstein; however, there is debate about the validity to that claim. Regardless, the sentiment in this statement is clear, compounding is powerful and the earlier you start, the bigger your end result. I reference compounding in the first part of this book related to your mindset and the behaviors to follow. Well, those behaviors applied financially will grow, sometimes exponentially of your initial investment.

Discipline is really key to financial success in the long-term. Discipline is important because it almost solidifies the establishment of routine that takes the thought out of doing what's right. Your actions become almost reflex-like, which keeps the temptation to deviate at bay. All of the strategies discussed in this book, require discipline. Discipline doesn't mean doing it right every time either, it's doing it consistently over time. So you break budget one week, so what. Next week get back and do better. When establishing discipline, many times people will get frustrated when they fall off. We're all human and prone to messing up. The success is in recognizing the deviation and then getting back on that horse and correcting it.

"Eventually you'll find whatever requires effort and discipline will become effortless once you've established the habit."
—RAHKIM SABREE

The key to adhering to goals is to not look for the temporary gain associated with realizing success and the early stages of progress, but instead, focus on enjoying your journey more than the destination itself.

"It's easy to fall off the bike, just make sure you get up and start pedaling again."
—RAHKIM SABREE

The Effects of a Lack of Planning and Universal Law

What does not having a long-term plan or discipline cost us? Most individuals impacted by poverty, or those who still have the Poverty Mindset make financial decisions out of a reflex for survival rather than being intentional savers or spenders. It's always "barely making ends meet" with no finish line in sight. There's a quote out there that goes something like, "When we don't know where we're going, everywhere will look the same." Which basically means you'll likely keep going in circles financially with no set goals or accomplishments because you haven't established a long-term plan or discipline around how to accomplish those plans.

The aspect of compounding that makes it so powerful is TIME. So long-term planning really leverages this idea to predict and often realize growth over time. By failing to have the long-term plan or discipline, you essentially lose out on the benefits associated with tapping into that compounding force. This can apply to brushing your teeth, working out, saving, investing, retirement, even succession or estate planning.

Making Emotional Financial Decisions

We're all prone to making knee-jerk or emotional decisions around anything financial. I can give an example: Markets are cyclical. We see them go up and go down. Within the discipline of investing and saving in the way that I do, I allocate a specific amount of my income toward saving and investing every time I get paid. I allocate these monies every time, regardless of what the circumstances are and where the market is. I do this to take advantage of what's called dollar cost averaging. Dollar cost averaging is a strategy that basically takes the sting out of volatility in the stock market. In that way, it's easy for me to take advantage of the dips in price and the benefits of increases in price in terms of value because I kept investing. Many people see a stock decreasing in value and immediately sell due to fear of loss. Stay the course!

"My plan is to focus on long-term growth and discipline, and not pay attention to my emotional reactions to what the market is doing today, but to consistently allocate that specific portion or more of my income toward investing and savings."

—RAHKIM SABREE

Discipline in Steps

"Rome wasn't built in a day."

You have to chip away with your process very slowly over time. For me, establishing discipline looks like deciding you need to wake up at 5am to get work done. Just waking up at 5am every day is the first step, but that doesn't mean you necessarily get out of bed at 5am. After a while, that discipline kind of takes hold of you and you slowly start to say, "Okay, at 5am, I'm going to actually get out of my bed." By getting out of the bed at 5am every day, you eventually work your way through small incremental steps to get to a point where you can go outside and leave the house and go to the gym, or read a book, or do yoga. That example is a testament to the idea of making small incremental changes that eventually snowball.

"Compounding can be demonstrated in EVERY aspect of your life."

—RAHKIM SABREE

Maybe you decide you can afford to put twenty dollars a pay period into a savings account. Then you realize you can do fifty or one-hundred dollars. Pretty soon you start to get excited that you can find extra money to put away and the next thing you know you're putting away thirty percent of your income without missing a beat. Guess what? You've already started the wheels turning by reading this book. You just have to start to take deliberate action.

P.S. Guys, I really want to see your progress. Please don't hesitate to share pictures, videos, posts about your progress on social media. Tag me, mention me, send me a DM, hashtag #FinanciallyIrresponsible so I can keep up.

"Applying compounding is really the first step in making effective long-term plans and disciplines, start TODAY. Take your first step in your ideal direction and always put one foot in front of the other until you get to a point where you start running or soaring."

—RAHKIM SABREE

CHAPTER 11
WHO WANTS TO RETIRE ANYWAYS?

Retirement and Financial Freedom

WHEN PEOPLE THINK ABOUT RETIREMENT, they often think of enjoying their time NOT working. They think of a beach house, traveling, spending time with the family, etc., but why can't we live that way now? Retirement is often coupled with a fixed income, limited spending, and sometimes boredom because someone may not know what to do with the free time they have. Retirement seems to be the most exciting for people who are working on someone else's dream. Some of the most successful and wealthy business owners in the world work until their last breath.

"Retirement is not the goal, financial freedom is."
—RAHKIM SABREE

However, some people's definition of financial freedom is having passive income be greater than your expenses, so in that way you're not trading time for money. Trading time for money is a very popular concept in the financial world. Most frequently it's applied to getting up and having to work for money. That's work either for yourself or someone else.

"The goal is to get to a place where your assets are generating enough income for you to have your time, so you can spend your time how you want to. Whether that be dedicating your time to a cause, fulfilling your life's purpose, or even chilling, traveling, or spending time with family and friends."

—RAHKIM SABREE

The Seduction of Retirement

In my opinion, TIME is the aspect of retirement that people are most attracted to. Not having to wake up in the morning, get dressed and go to somebody's job for eight-nine-ten hours per day is an appealing idea for many people.

There's this whole movement called the 'FIRE Movement' where people are looking to retire much earlier than what is considered traditional. Fire stands for "Financial Independence Retire Early," and it comes from the Dave Ramsey school of thought. It has become a culture that's established around people finding ways to aggressively save, and invest early-on, to eliminate debt and live off of the money they've accumulated. There's often a very strict and aggressive method of limiting expenses that is even more so aggressive than my own methods.

The Problem with Early Retirement

The problem a lot of people face by retiring early is that they are limited to whatever income their assets are producing. Or they have limited longevity up to a certain point once they've exhausted their wealth. In those situations, a person would have to live a very modest lifestyle, which isn't a problem. But someone would need to ask themselves, is that the lifestyle they want to live? Did you work as hard as you did to put away as much as you did so that you can continue to live a very minimalist lifestyle? Or do you want to be able to splurge a little bit and relax?

I personally subscribe to the idea of using leverage and accumulating good debt that's going to produce income through assets which many in the Dave Ramsey school of thought deeply oppose.

In whatever approach you take, financial independence and having more time to yourself is a theme to be considered. The idea of retirement is not really speaking to not doing anything all day, but instead ... being able to dictate what you want to do with your time, which financial freedom will afford you.

401k All Day?

I think the financial services industry has done a really good job at marketing the 401k as the go-to product for retirement. A lot of millennial and gen-z workers aren't familiar with the concept of a pension, which the 401k replaced in many lines of work.

So I think it's important for people to understand the origins of the 401k and why it was implemented and widely accepted by employers. There was a shift from employers having the responsibility to dole out income for tenure that their previous employees had over the period of their retirement, to now putting the onus on the employees to put enough money away so that they can support themselves in retirement.

The 401k is the most popular type of employer-sponsored retirement plan. It is advertised as being the savings vehicle for retirement. The way it works is simple enough; you divert a portion of your salary on a pre-tax basis (unless it's a Roth 401k) into an account often accompanied by a company match up to a certain percentage or amount.

With the 401k, YOU are in the driver's seat with how much you contribute and how consistently you contribute. However, beware. There's also this not-so-widely-known fact that 401k plans have hidden management fees which eat at your overall gains. In Killing Secret Cows by Garrett B. Gunderson, he introduces and debunks some of the myths associated with the 401k. I personally believe that the 401k is a tool people should absolutely take advantage of. Especially if your company is giving you a generous match. However, I do not recommend the 401k as the ultimate retirement planning vehicle. In fact, I don't recommend any one product as the ultimate retirement vehicle. It's a tool like any other that when properly utilized can yield fantastic results.

"People should be proactive in getting the facts first before handing over the reins to somebody else to manage their funds when they have the option to do it themselves."

—Rahkim Sabree

My Experience with the 401K

As I shared earlier, I personally stopped contributing to my 401k because of a variety of factors, some I've outlined, others I haven't. I do invest though and in doing so I have the option to invest in whatever it is that I want to. You see, your options are limited in a 401k. You have the option to choose from several funds within a plan that your employer has selected for you. I'm a bit of a control freak when it comes to money and I like to have all the power to make choices as I see fit. This is my preference; you may have another.

I have leveraged many of the benefits the 401k has to offer as a tool for investing. Again, I don't plan on using my 401k to fund my entire retirement. When I speak to people about the 401k, I share with them that it's very likely their 401k is NOT going to fund their entire retirement alone. One of the benefits I've been able to take advantage of is borrowing against my 401k, which in my opinion is a far better option than making a premature withdrawal, paying taxes on that withdrawal as income, and being penalized for the early withdrawal. What's nice about borrowing against the 401k is that when you take that loan and you start paying it back, you're paying that loan back with interest to yourself. Which means, that is money that's going back to you.

The 401k also serves as a tax benefit for people who earn

high incomes. Your contributions to the 401k are pre-tax contributions and basically what that means is, if there's a certain portion of your income that you put into your 401k over the course of the year, when you go to file your taxes, you're able to claim less now on after tax income than the amount you earned over that year. This is huge as you can effectively lower your tax liability simply by stashing away in your 401k. Though, you do pay taxes on that money on withdrawal at retirement age.

I also mentioned the option for a Roth 401k, which is a newer product that allows you to contribute on a post-tax basis. Meaning, you pay taxes first on the money so that only after-tax dollars go in. The benefit of this is that when you pull the money out, you're not paying taxes on any money that you pull out, including any gains that money has made while sitting and accumulating.

There are also two retirement account types that I want to mention here separate from the 401k. That is the Traditional IRA and the Roth IRA. Both of these account types are built for saving with similar rules and advantages to the 401k, except they are not employer funded, they have contribution limits for the year, and also income limits that dictate your ability to contribute. I would recommend exploring in depth the different vehicles listed here as well as the 403B, SEP IRA, and Simple IRA.

I have contributed to both types of 401ks and both types of IRAs. I recommend just starting SOMEWHERE. You can always adjust. A general rule is that whatever your company is matching up to, you do the same if you can afford to. Just don't let that be the ONLY way you plan for retirement.

By the way, you should understand how to leverage the tax benefits of contributing to these vehicles for retirement. Have a consultation with a CPA or tax accountant.

"The 401k is a great tool if you understand how it works."

—RAHKIM SABREE

Retirement Tool-HSA

The HSA is a tool I've recently learned about myself. It's a tool to plan for retirement healthcare expenses with tax deferred benefits. So you can contribute in the same way that you can to a traditional 401k, pre-tax, to an HSA. The HSA is a health savings account with maximums during the year (similar to the IRA). You can use the money that you contribute to that plan, tax-free, for qualified medical expenses. This is huge benefit because it doesn't expire, and it can travel with you from company to company. Some companies even provide wellness incentives that equate to contributions on your behalf for performing wellness activities like preventative health screenings (more free money!). One thing I really like about the HAS is that you can invest the money that's in there just like you can in an IRA or 401k.

The reason I highlight HSA's as being an important part of long-term planning, specifically retirement planning, is because when you're young, on average, you're pretty healthy. You're not visiting the doctor often, so you don't need to spend so much on health care expenses. But because of that, most people don't think about the fact that health care expenses are not a matter of "if" but a matter of "when" and so it's definitely inevitable. If you can start saving now on a tax-free basis over long periods of time for healthcare expenses that are inevitable, that's hugely ideal. You are absolutely going to have health expenses at some point or another. If not for you, maybe for someone in your family. If you start saving now, you have already started to plan for a financial expense you would be hit with later on in life. Having a budget allocated for expenses that you didn't consider is a wise financial decision. By not having money saved before, you will have to pay for unexpected expenses out of pocket instead of using your allocated savings.

HSA Account Hack

Try investing the funds. Allow that money to grow, leveraging the concept of compounding over time while continuing to contribute toward it. Any growth occurring over time that you've been contributing toward, whether it be dividend reinvestment, interests, or employer contribution, would enable you to have more at your disposal in terms of money allocated for healthcare expenses. Even though you've decreased your taxable income by making these pre-tax contributions to the plan, you're still saving or contributing a certain portion of your own income to saving overtime, which is very important. Like I said, I don't think one should be opposed to saving or planning for the future.

"Someone should have several different financial vehicles that they take advantage of."

—Rahkim Sabree

CHAPTER 12
GENERATIONAL WEALTH

"If you want to go fast go alone, if you want to go far go together"

Defining Generational Wealth

WHY IS GENERATIONAL WEALTH SO important? For me, generational wealth is more than the transferring of assets to future generations. Generational wealth speaks more to legacy building. It gives future generations a head-start where they can build for themselves on the previous generations' foundation. Passing down generational wealth means that the next generation doesn't have to play catch-up, which is frequently the case in so-called minority communities. They don't know any better. They don't know how to preserve wealth and pass that wealth on to additional generations, or maybe they don't even have a desire to do so.

"Ultimately, having generational wealth means your children are not playing catch-up to opportunities they may have missed out on, or couldn't have taken advantage of, because they don't have a foundation to refer to."

—RAHKIM SABREE

Student loan debt garners national attention as being a huge financial issue. A big reason why people have to take out student loans is because they don't have wealth to tap into to cover the cost of going to school.

Student Loans

It's almost become a bad word in today's society. I'd always been a pretty bright student. I maintained honor roll status from the time I was in kindergarten up through high school. However, this was a double-edged sword. You see, I never really had to apply myself. School came so easy to me that I was coasting through on cruise control. I failed my first class ever during my sophomore year in high school because I literally did nothing. I showed up, I wrote my first name on a piece of paper and I zoned out. I'm telling you this story because when it became time for me to start applying for college, I was already playing catch up. I had no idea where I wanted to go and, quite frankly, who would accept me. I also didn't have the experience of my parents to guide that process. It was all very last minute. I got three acceptance letters and two with awards. The two with awards were private colleges and the tuition was expensive. I visited the less expensive of the two schools and was under-enthused. However, it was impressed upon me by someone that I should go away to college (not community college which would have been free for me) and if I didn't like it, I could always transfer out after the first year. I was also told that I should not worry about student loans because "everyone has student loans." I took this advice and blindly signed all the papers for the loan.

The first year of school, I had no money. My supplies and toiletries came from the nearest dollar store, I used spare change to make copies of the pages of textbooks I needed, and I manage to survive that first year carrying mostly Cs and a D. I share this story because too often young people are thrust into college and university campuses with this carefree and naïve mentality around the weight student loan debt carries with it, until it's too late. After that first year, I did transfer out, to the local community college where my education was free. Part of being financially responsible parents, uncles, aunts, brothers, sisters, mentors, friends, etc. is shedding light on the financial mishaps and burdens we have experienced to prevent the next generation from making the same mistakes.

The Importance of Financial Literacy and Heirs to the Throne

Beyond the passing of resources, it's important to pass on financial knowledge, so future generations can become financially literate. Financial literacy is important to know not only for your own financial journey, but also for the people who come after you. Your journey of wealth building can begin with having good credit and maintaining good credit all throughout your life. You could have a healthy retirement and savings plan. You could have good spending and budgeting habits. But along your financial journey, you can get to a point where you can't take care of yourself anymore, or you're no longer here, which means your family is now left with the burden of tying up loose ends to your estate.

If you didn't pass the knowledge of financial literacy you've learned onto your heirs, then they're starting from zero, from a knowledge perspective. They may have access to all of the resources, accounts, and benefits from all you've built. But those heirs are very quickly going to lose it because they don't have the content knowledge to know how to manage it.

"The true wealth is in your ability to share knowledge and resources to future generations."

—Rahkim Sabree

Generational Wealth and Celebrities

I do not plan on dying anytime soon; what are the advantages of me thinking about my wills, trusts and business entities? Using some cultural examples is a great way to answer this question. With the artist Prince, who died without a will or trust established, there was a lot of fighting amongst his family members about who would get what he left behind with his massive estate. With the artist Aretha Franklin, the same situation occurred where she passed away without a will. She had wealth left behind, and it was unclear as to where that wealth should have been directed.

Long Term Planning and Financial Decisions

From my varied experience working with people in financial services, I've seen a lot of ugliness that comes with not planning for death. I've seen some really savvy people who come in and have very detailed trusts that talk about what they want to have happen with their wealth, how they want to distribute it, and who they want controlling it. Wealth is relative, right? Wealth could be $50,000. Wealth could be $50 million. People having a plan for what happens with the money or assets they leave behind is what matters. So it's important to start thinking about that now. Because now, your soul, mind, and body are able to make those financial decisions and you can willingly and consciously choose who you want to be the backup for making those decisions for you. You get to determine and dictate what happens with specific financial variables, and if you want your wealth to skip a generation, or at what point you want your wealth to start being allocated.

Since we can't time death, it's important to plan now, because you can turn around something tragic can happen to you overnight or at any point in time. You want to have those financial details planned ahead of time. You don't want your family to be caught up in a situation where they fight over what is yours for their benefit.

Positioning Oneself for Generational Wealth

How does one best set themselves up for generational wealth? You need to establish a team. Your team could include key heirs, your CPA, and an attorney who specializes in estate planning, and have them walk you through the process of leaving behind wealth. They can walk you through and advise you on what the process will be when you pass away. They'll likely make recommendations as far as limiting liability from a tax perspective on your heirs, but also from a risk perspective, in terms of exposure or even privacy.

Again, you don't know what you don't know. So consulting with people like a CPA or attorney are crucial for protecting you and what you've built and will build in the future. Be proactive. Think how you can protect your money as it comes, or even before it comes, so that when it does happen, you're ready to execute immediately.

Life Insurance

The last comment I have is that you should start planning by getting life insurance. Again, death can strike at any time. If you are in control of any assets like a house, you definitely want to have a life insurance policy that will provide coverage of those assets and any funeral expenses you may leave your family to deal with. Shortly after purchasing my house, I took out a policy. With life insurance, my mortgage will be able to be paid off, along with whatever expenses that are associated with my burial. It's morbid to think about; however, it's necessary. Give your family, or whoever you designate as beneficiary, peace of mind knowing you have it covered. I know I've declared multiple times over that the content of this book is not financial advice, however, I implore you to research a life insurance policy as an immediate call to action beyond meeting with an attorney and/or CPA. A licensed professional will likely be able to assist you in determining the right policy for you, as well as taking out a policy that will cover your debts, assets, and obviously take care of your family.

CHAPTER 13
PAYING IT FORWARD

"You do not belong to you. You belong to the Universe.
Your significance will remain forever obscure to you, but
you may assume that you are fulfilling your role if you apply
yourself to converting your experiences to the
highest advantage of others."

—BUCKMINSTER FULLER

Defining Paying it Forward

PAYING IT FORWARD IS TAKING advantage of opportunities and being able to provide and share those same benefits and opportunities with somebody else. Paying it forward is more than important, it's a requirement.

With the current financial system, navigating it is not something taught in public educational institutions. I personally don't believe it ever will be because it would change the thread by which we weave the workforce, not only in this country but around the world.

Rising Entrepreneurs and Financial Empowerment

Author Robert Kiyosaki talks about how the western system of education is designed to produce two types of people: soldiers and employees; people who take orders. So with the rise and popularity of entrepreneurship, there's certainly a shift occurring where people want to control their own destiny, financially or otherwise. People are applying their skills from a variety of different places, including the traditional labor force to working on things that matter to them. Whether it be starting their own organizations, or building businesses from the ground up, there is certainly a sense of satisfaction involved in determining on your own the value you can provide in a particular space. I think it's important to pay it forward because it's a powerful form of charity. It's a way to mentor. It's a way to give back. You can definitely help someone who may not have had the same opportunities you were afforded and put them on a path toward creating their own opportunities in the same way you were able to.

> *"Financial empowerment is a team sport. Leveraging different individuals such as a mentor or different professionals you interact with, a wealth manager, financial advisor, an accountant, an attorney, a real estate agent, a lender, etc. They all play an integral role in shaping what is ultimately your financial destiny, your financial future."*
>
> —Rahkim Sabree

As a result of having a financial team, you get to pull from all of their expertise and sort and sift through the mistakes, learning moments, and successes. As a result, you can change and accelerate your processes so you don't become derailed. With paying it forward, you can share advice with someone else, so they can run with it and build on the foundation you have laid out.

> *"A key component to maintaining and facilitating the transfer of generational wealth is being able to pay it forward from a knowledge perspective in ways in which you've learned to best navigate financial systems and processes."*
>
> —Rahkim Sabree

Why Paying it Forward is a Requirement

A social cause that is near and dear to me is homelessness. I co-founded a non-profit in 2018 that focuses on addressing homelessness from a preventive perspective by educating people on a variety of things that include health and wellness best practices, employment development, and mentoring (for more information visit www.aeh-ct. org). We also focus on financial education by sharing how someone can become financially empowered, understand how to budget, how to save, and know which strategies to apply. Homelessness has been drawing more and more attention, becoming an national and international issue, or an epidemic in this country. If you close your eyes and imagine what someone who is homeless looks like, that image almost always never looks like you.

Why?

What separates working-class citizens from individuals impacted by homelessness? Maybe a paycheck or two. One of my missions through this organization is to create awareness around the spectrum of homelessness and how truly close to home it is. We often don't realize how close we are to homelessness.

"This person chose to be homeless"

"That person is lazy"

"Get a job!"

"That person is a drug addict"

Are all things the media might teach you to say about those impacted by homelessness when really there are a variety of factors that lead into why somebody is homeless.

Homelessness is literally right under your nose. If you go to your average urban high school, there will most certainly be statistics to demonstrate this. I went and gave a talk at a local high school and the staff quoted statistics saying, "The school was aware that twenty percent of their high school students were homeless and couldn't do anything about it." Hearing a statistic like that, you realize that homelessness extends far beyond the smelly guy asking you for change and a warm meal to teenagers who are couch-surfing from one friend's house to the next. There is a whole population of individuals who go off to college and become homeless. You read my story; fortunately, I was able to secure a loan but what if I hadn't or something happened and I couldn't make it home, then what? Once I mentored someone who was several years younger than me on and off again over the course of some years. He was away at school and one day out of the blue I felt inclined to ask, "Are you ok?" He shared that he was sleeping in the bus station. He was hours from home, and he didn't have a place to stay so he slept in the bus station overnight and then went to school early in the morning to take a shower, change his clothes, and go to class.

I sent him small amount of money over the period of maybe a month, tried to offer him support from the perspective of identifying resources, instructing him toward different places he could go, different numbers he can call in order to get himself out of that situation. He was so dedicated to finishing school and doing well in his classes that he just allowed himself to be homeless in the interim while he was trying to figure out his situation. He stayed in shelters. He was jumped. He was robbed. All this happened to a kid trying to go to college and get an education. Sadly, this situation is not unique to him. Eventually, I'm happy to say, he was able to secure housing and continue his studies uninterrupted. Talk about dedication!

Paying it forward is a component, a requirement, an obligation for people who learn how to navigate these systems. They can go out and share what they know so other people who are negatively impacted or at risk of being impacted by things like homelessness can have a fighting chance.

Paying it Forward, Personal Character, Legacy Building

I've benefited by building relationships with people who can in turn pay back what I've paid them in the future when they get to their destination. To me, paying it forward to somebody else is the greatest gift because I'm able to impact others as a result of work I do. Paying it forward speaks to someone's character, legacy, and efforts. But in order to pay it forward, you have to make sure you get yourself straight first, and so that's the intention of this body of work. You can't pour from an empty cup, and the best way to help someone else is to help yourself first.

If you've even been on an airplane and they're going through the evacuation procedures. When they show passengers the masks, the first thing they tell you is "Make sure that you all put your mask on before you try to help somebody else." I think that message is important to apply in all areas of life, especially when it comes to finances. If you're not doing well, and you try to help, you're not doing them a favor, and you're certainly not doing yourself a favor because now you're both in a situation where you're in need.

Financially Empowering Yourself and Others

Some ways people can pay it forward would be to really take the content that I'm sharing to heart, and let it inspire a spark and desire in you to learn more. My strongest encouragement is that people go out and learn more, understand the terms that I've used, and understand the products that I've referred to. Understand how they work to your advantage or disadvantage. Learn as much as you possibly can. But also, share or buy this book for somebody, share your copy with someone so they can also learn. Continue to invest in yourself, take on the responsibility to change, and hold yourself accountable. You can take all the knowledge you absorb and not do anything with it, and it's not going to serve you in any way by keeping it all in your head.

There's a quote that's circulating on social media, it resonates with me and I'd like to share with you. "If you didn't come from a wealthy family, a wealthy family must come from you."

"I believe that everybody can be empowered to build wealth if they understand money."

—Rahkim Sabree

When YOU Become Wealthy, Remember to Pay it Forward

A lot of what I've talked about in this text is foundational for getting to a point where you can build momentum around increasing wealth. I will also remind you of the Bible story that I opened this book with: the text about the ten talents that exist in Matthew. Don't bury that talent, multiply it.

> "The secret that most people miss is that wealth building is not about getting more money. Getting more money is a byproduct of wealth building. Wealth building is about creating systems and implementing or executing strategies that give you the opportunity to live your best life. Wealth building gives you the opportunity and the capacity to walk in your purpose, and stop having to trade your time for money, so that you can focus on things that matter the most. Because at the end of the day, your money doesn't go with you."
>
> —RAHKIM SABREE

Beyond Money, Legacy

The last example I have is a cultural reference to Steve Jobs, the co-founder and face of Apple products. At one time, he was one of the richest men in the world, and he realized his mortality as he was dying from pancreatic cancer. His company continued on and became the first trillion-dollar company in the world, years after he died. But none of those achievements changed his mortality or changed the fact that he was subject to the human elements of life, just like everybody else. A person may get to the point where they acquire wealth and have the ability to do and have whatever they want ... but that's not what's important.

"What's important is being able to live out your life and share your experiences, successes, and freedom with other people you care about, and people that care about you."

By paying it forward, you grow your network of people who will care about you, or who will speak fondly of you, and who will remember you when you are ultimately gone. When you pay it forward you will be remembered as somebody who impacted and changed not only their life, but the lives of everybody else you were able to touch.

GLOSSARY OF FINANCIAL TERMS

401 (K) Plan – tax-advantaged, defined-contribution retirement account offered by employers to their employees. Named after a section of the U.S. Internal Revenue Code. Investment not taxed until employee withdraws money.

403 (B) Plan – a retirement account for certain employees of public schools and tax-exempt organizations. Similar to a 401 (k) plan specific to employees of public schools and tax-exempt organizations rather than private-sector workers.

80-20 Rule – (also known as the Pareto principle) An aphorism, which asserts that 80% of outcomes (or outputs) result from 20% of all causes (or inputs) for a given event.

Asset — a resource with economic value than an individual, corporation or country owns or controls with the expectation that it will provide a future benefit. (something that can generate cash flow, reduce expenses, or improve sales)

ATM Card — A card that allows you access to funds via an ATM. Not to be confused with a debit card which allows you access to funds via an ATM AND allows you to make purchases via debits.

Budget — an estimation of revenue and expenses over a specified future period of time and is usually compiled and re-evaluated on a periodic basis. (A financial plan for a defined period)

Capitalism — An economic system in which private individuals or businesses own capital goods. The production of goods and services is based on supply and demand in the general market.

Compounding (Compound Interest) — Interest calculated on the initial principal, which also includes all of the accumulated interest of previous periods of a deposit or loan.

Corporation — A corporation is a legal entity that is separate and distinct from its owners. Corporations enjoy most of the rights and responsibilities that individuals possess; they can enter contracts, loan and borrow money, sue and be sued, hire employees, own assets and pay taxes.

Credit — Generally defined as a contractual agreement in which a borrower receives something of value now and agrees to repay the lender at a later date with interest.

Credit Card — A card that lets holders borrow funds with which to pay for goods and services. Credit cards impose the condition that cardholders pay back the borrowed money, plus interest, as well as any additional agreed-upon charges.

Credit Limit — The maximum amount of credit a financial institution extends to a client. A lending institution extends a credit limit on a credit card or a line of credit.

Credit Report — A credit report is a detailed break down of an individual's credit history prepared by a credit bureau. Lenders use the reports created based on that information, along with other details to determine loan applicant's creditworthiness.

Credit Score — A statistical number that evaluates a consumer's creditworthiness and is based on credit history. Lenders use credit scores to evaluate the probability that an individual will repay his or her debts. A person's credit score ranges from 300-850, the higher the score, the more financially trustworthy a person is considered to be.

DDA (Demand Deposit Account) — An account that consist of funds held in a bank account from which deposited funds can be withdrawn at any time, such as checking accounts.

Debit Card — A payment card that deducts money directly from a consumer's checking account to pay for a purchase. Also called check cards, debit cards eliminate the need to carry cash or physical checks to make purchases. (Pressing 'credit' on a debit transaction doesn't make the card a credit card or build your credit).

Debt — an amount of money borrowed by one party from another. Used as a method of making large purchases that could not otherwise be afforded under normal circumstances. A debt arrangement gives the borrowing party permission to borrow money under the condition that it is to be paid back at a later date, usually with interest.

Debt-to-Income Ratio — The debt-to-income (DTI) ratio is a personal finance measure that compares an individual's monthly debt payment to his or her monthly gross income. Your gross income is your pay before taxes and other deductions are taken out. The debt-to-income ration is the percentage of your gross monthly income that goes to paying your monthly debt payments.

Dividend — the distribution of reward from a portion of the company's earnings and is paid to a class of its shareholders.

Dividend Reinvestment Program (Plan) (DRIP) – a program that allows investors to reinvest their cash dividends into additional shares or fractional shares of the underlying stock on the dividend payment date.

Diversification — refers to a risk management strategy that mixes a wide variety of investments within a portfolio. The aim is to smooth out unsystematic risk events in a portfolio, so the positive performance of some investments neutralizes the negative performance of others.

Dollar-Cost Averaging — An investment strategy in which an investor divides up the total amount to be invested across periodic purchases of a target asset in an effort to reduce the impact of volatility on the overall purchase. The purchases occur regardless of the asset's price and at regular intervals. Also known as the constant dollar plan.

Dow Jones Industrial Average (DJIA) — An index that tracks 30 large, publicly owned companies trading on the New York Stock Exchange (NYSE) and the NASDAQ. When the TV networks say "the market is up today," they are generally referring to the Dow.

Equity (popular phrase "pay me in") — referred to as shareholder equity which represents the amount of money that would be returned to a company's shareholders if all of the assets were liquidated and all of the company's debt was paid off. (think of it as a degree of ownership in any asset after subtracting all debts associated with that asset)

Exchange Traded Funds (ETF) — a type of security that involves a collection of securities—such as stocks—that often tracks an underlying index. ETFs are in many ways similar to mutual funds; however, they are listed on exchanges and ETF shares trade throughout the day just like ordinary stock. (Well known example is SPDR S&P 500 ETF (SPY), which tracks the S&P 500 Index.)

Executor (or executrix) — of an estate is an individual appointed to administer the estate of a deceased person. The main duty is to carry out the instructions to manage the affairs and wishes of the deceased person's estate. Appointed by either the testator of the will (individual who makes the will), or by a court, in cases wherein there was no prior appointment.

Federal Deposit Insurance Corporation (FDIC) — an independent federal agency insuring deposits in the U.S. banks and thrifts in the event of bank failures. The FDIC insures deposits up to $250,000 per depositor as long as the institution is a member firm.

Federal Housing Administration (FHA) — A U.S. agency offering mortgage insurance to FHA-approved lenders that meet specific qualifications. Mortgage insurance protects lenders against losses from mortgage defaults.

Financial Independence, Retire Early (FIRE) — a movement dedicated to the program of extreme savings and investment that allows proponents to retire far earlier than traditional budgets and retirement plans would allow. (By dedicating up to 70% of income to savings, followers of the FIRE movement may eventually be able to quite their jobs and live solely off small withdrawals from their portfolios)

Financial Industry Regulatory Authority (FINRA) — an independent, nongovernmental organization that writes and enforces the rules governing registered brokers and broker-dealer firms in the United States. Its stated mission is "to safeguard the investing public against fraud and bad practices."

Financial Literacy — the education and understanding of various financial areas including topics related to managing personal finance, money and investing.

Group Economics — a group of people with a common

economic interest who agree to actively and consciously pursue that economic interest together.

Guarantor (re: Student loans/Co-signer/Business credit) — a person who guarantees to pay a borrower's debt in the event the borrow defaults on a loan obligation. A guarantor acts as co-signer.

Health Savings Account (HSA) — a tax-advantaged account created for individuals who are covered under high-deductible health plans. Contributions are made by the individual or their employer and are limited to a maximum amount each year. The contributions can be invested over time and can be used to pay for qualified medical expenses.

Home Equity (Loan or Line of Credit) — Home equity is the value of the homeowner's interest in their home. A home equity loan or line of credit (HELOC) is a second mortgage on the house that allows homeowners to borrow against their equity.

Index Fund — a type of mutual fund with a portfolio constructed to match or track the components of a financial market index such as the S&P 500.

Individual Retirement Account (IRA) (see ROTH and Traditional) — a tax-advantaged investing tool that individuals use to earmark funds for retirement savings.

Inflation — a quantitative measure of the rate at which the average price level of a basket of selected goods and services in an economy increase over time in comparison to the decrease in purchasing power of a nation's currency.

Interest Rate — The amount a lender charges for the use of assets expressed as a percentage of the principal.

Irrevocable Trust — a type of trust where its terms cannot be modified, amended or terminated without the permission of the grantor's named beneficiary or beneficiaries. The grantor, having effectively transferred all ownership of assets into the trust, legally removes their rights of ownerships to the assets and the trust.

Liability — Items or services purchased that take money out of your pockets. The ideal order of operations is Purchase (Assets) to then purchase (Liabilities).

Life Insurance — Life insurance is a contract between an insurer and a policyholder in which the insurer guarantees payment of a death benefit to the named beneficiaries upon the death of the insured.

Liquidity — Liquidity describes the degree to which an asset or security can be quickly bought or sold in the market at a price reflecting its intrinsic value.

Limited Liability Company (LLC) — a corporate structure in the US whereby the owners are not personally liable for the company's debts or liabilities. LLC's are hybrid entities that combine the characteristics of a corporation with those of a partnership or sole proprietorship.

Money Market Account — an interest bearing account at a bank or credit union and often include check writing and debit card privileges. Money Markets are similar to savings accounts in that they pay interest and have transaction limitations per month.

Multilevel Marketing — is a strategy some direct sales companies use to encourage existing distributors to recruit new distributors who are paid a percentage of their recruits' sales. The recruits are the distributor's "down line".

Mutual Fund — a type of financial vehicle made up of a pool of money collected from many investors to invest in securities like stocks, bonds, money market instruments, and other assets.

Network Marketing — a business model that depends on person-to-person sales by independent representatives, often working from home. A network marketing business can be a single-tier program, whereby you sell the products or multi-tier where you recruit salespeople. (see MLM)

Not for Profit — a type of organization that does not earn profits for its owners. All of the money earned by or donated to the not-for-profit organization is used in pursuing the organization's objectives and keeping it running. They are typically tax-exempt charities or a type of public service organization.

Overdraft — an extension of credit from a lending institution that is granted when an account reaches zero. Typically, when a bank account is over drafted there is a fee associated.

Partnership — A formal arrangement by two or more parties to manage and operate a business and share its profits.

PayDay Loans — a type of short-term borrowing where a lender will extend high-interest credit based on a borrower's income and credit profile.

Ponzi Scheme — a fraudulent investing scam promising high rates of return with little risk to investors. The Ponzi scheme generates returns for early investors by acquiring new investors. This is similar to a pyramid scheme in that both are based on using new investors' funds to pay the earlier backers. Ponzi schemes and pyramid schemes eventually bottom out when the flood of new investors dries up and there isn't enough money to go around.

Real Estate Investment Trust (REIT) — a company owning and typically operating real estate which generates income.

Refinance — occurs when an individual or business revises the interest rate, payment schedule, and terms of a previous credit agreement. Debtors will often choose to refinance a loan agreement when the interest rate environment has substantially changed, causing potential savings on debt payments from a new agreement.

Roth IRA — IRA the reverse of a traditional IRA. After-tax dollars are contributed which can then be invested and grow tax free once you take the money out. Don't have a minimum distribution requirement and can be passed along to heirs if not used.

S&P 500 Index (Standard & Poor's 500 Index) — a market capitalization weighted index of the 500 largest U.S. publicly traded companies.

S-Corp (also known as an S Subchapter) — refers to a type of corporation that meets specific Internal Revenue Code requirements. The requirements give a corporation with 100 shareholders of less the benefit of incorporation while being taxed as a partnership. This corporation may pass income directly to shareholders and avoid double taxation.

Stock — a type of security that signifies proportionate ownership in the issuing corporation. (see, ownership/ equity)

Term Life Insurance — Is life insurance that guarantees payment of a stated death benefit during a specified term. Once the term expires, the policyholder can either renew it for another term, convert the policy to permanent coverage, or allow the policy to terminate.

Traditional IRA — IRA's where you can put pre-tax income into investments of your choice, which grow tax-deferred until you withdraw the money.

Trust — a fiduciary relationship in which one party, known as a trustor, gives another party, the trustee, the right to hold title to property or assets for the benefit of a third party, the beneficiary.

Trustee — a person or firm that holds and administers property or assets for the benefit of a third party.

Universal Life Insurance — permanent life insurance with an investment savings element and low premiums like term life insurance.

Whole Life Insurance — provides coverage for the life of the insured. In addition to providing a death benefit, whole life also contains a savings component where cash value may accumulate.

APPENDIX/ RESOURCES

Website resources:

- CreditKarma.com
- annualcreditreport.com
- DaveRamsey.com
- RahkimSabree.com
- Bettermoneyhabits.com
- Finra.org

Books:

- Rich Dad Poor Dad
- Tax-Free Wealth

- Richest Man in Babylon
- Think and Grow Rich
- The Millionaire Next Door
- Money Master the Game
- The Compound Effect
- The Seven Habits of Highly Effective People
- The Law of Attraction
- Killing Sacred Cows
- The Intelligent Investor
- The Power of Habit
- Post Traumatic Slave Syndrome

ABOUT THE AUTHOR

RAHKIM SABREE IS A 2x author, public speaker, and educator in the personal finance space. His goal is to hone-in on the things that make people think and feel empowered. His passion for the topics he writes about are evident in the words he chooses to use in sharing not only his message, but his experiences. He grew up in Mount Vernon, NY and graduated from Mount Vernon High School.

In addition to being an author and public speaker, Rahkim has turned his efforts to social causes, co-founding a not-for-profit in 2018 called An Extended Hand, Inc. The non-profit aims to address homelessness and education gaps in the community by focusing program around financial education, collaborative growth, individualized holistic care, and employment development for the working poor, those impacted by homelessness, those at risk of homelessness, and at-risk youth. For more information on his nonprofit and their efforts visit **www.AEH-ct.org**.

For more information on Rahkim Sabree directly visit **www.RahkimSabree.com**